THE FUTURE
OF THE
AMERICAN
FAMILY

THE FUTURE
OF THE
AMERICAN FAMILY

GEORGE BARNA

MOODY PRESS
CHICAGO

Scripture taken from the HOLY BIBLE, NEW KING JAMES VERSION®. Copyright © 1982 by Thomas
Nelson, Inc. All rights reserved.

Interior design and charts by William Paetzold.

Produced for Moody Press by the Livingstone Corporation. James C. Galvin, Ed.D., J. Michael Kendrick,
Darcy J. Kamps, project staff.

ISBN: 0-8024-2899-1
1 3 5 7 9 10 8 6 4 2
Printed in the United States of America

CONTENTS

Acknowledgments
9

Preface
11

Note to the Reader
15

CHAPTER 1
The Cleavers Don't Live Here Anymore
Sweeping social and cultural challenges have battered the traditional family in America. People are reacting in fear and confusion to the changes swirling around them. Nevertheless, there are some surprising facts about the strength of our families that you won't hear from the media.
17

CHAPTER 2
The Nouveau Family
Americans today are defining their families in new, untraditional ways. Discover why this trend is popular—and why the implications are so alarming for Christian families.
25

CHAPTER 3
Marriage Is Alive and Well
We hear from experts and the press that marriage is a dying institution. Yet, as our research reveals, marriage remains as strong as ever, despite the pressures of modern life.
39

88546

CHAPTER 4
The Truth About Divorce
The hard facts about divorce may be quite different from what you're used to hearing. Our research shows that the common notions about divorce— "half of all marriages end in divorce," "divorce is liberating," "the children are least affected by a marital breakup"—are not supported by the evidence.

65

CHAPTER 5
Parenting Isn't Child's Play Anymore
Parents in America still love their kids, but they are having fewer of them. Our research sheds light on why parents are hesitant to have larger families. Also, we look at the "quality time/quantity time" debate.

93

CHAPTER 6
Single and Never Been Married
Young people today who have never been married are vastly different from previous generations. They wait longer to get married, cohabit more often, are more likely to reject traditional values, and even move in with their parents more frequently. Find out what is behind these trends.

119

CHAPTER 7
Homosexual Families
Despite the efforts of a vocal gay rights lobby, Americans are still uncomfortable with the idea of homosexual families. Also, our research shows that the actual number of homosexuals in the U. S. population is far less than the 10 percent figure trumpeted in the press.

143

CHAPTER 8
Minority Families
As black and Hispanic families make up an ever-increasing portion of the U.S. population, they exert a growing influence on our notions of family. Discover how their influence is shaping our culture.

157

CHAPTER 9
Making Time for Family

Americans are feeling more than ever the constraints of time on their family life.
Women who work outside the home are especially feeling the heat. Our research
reveals how they are holding up.

171

CHAPTER 10
Faith and Family

The declining influence of religion on American families is evident. Yet Americans
still retain a strong core of religious beliefs. Discover why churches have been slow to
respond to today's families—and how they can improve their track record.

187

CHAPTER 11
Strengthening Our Families

A fearsome array of challengers wants to dismantle the traditional family. Yet our
families possess remarkable staying power that can survive even these battles. Learn
how you can shore up your own relationships and persuade others to form a new
consensus that supports family values.

203

Acknowledgments

I am thankful to God for the people who care about me and support me in so many ways. I want to publicly thank those who have sacrificed themselves to help me develop and complete this book.

My team of colleagues at the Barna Research Group, Ltd., fully supported me in this endeavor. Cindy Coats, Keith Deaville, Gwen Ingram, Vibeke Klocke, George Maupin, Paul Rottler, Ron Sellers, and Telford Work have covered for me during my extended absences from the office and during my spacey moments while I was there. What a blessing it is to work with a group committed to each other, to truth, and to making a difference in the world.

Though my friends at Regal Books were disappointed about not having the opportunity to publish this book, they continued to provide me with information about the state of the American family. Their friendship, support, and example of how to be a shining light in a world of darkness is unique and something I cherish. I am especially indebted to Bill Greig III for his consistent encouragement and assistance in seeking to understand our culture, the church, and ways in which information can be made useful to those who serve Christ.

Other organizations and people have helped by providing information for this book. I thank the Family Research Council for quickly forwarding a series of research papers and suggesting other ideas to broaden my horizons on the issues. My thanks also go to John Court at Fuller Seminary for sharing his resources and contacts with me. It was wonderful having exposure to such experts.

I am also grateful to have worked with the team at Moody Press. Jim Bell in particular deserves my thanks as a respected colleague familiar with the travails of research, and as the person who believed enough in me to pursue this project. The marketing and editorial teams helped to improve the final product. May this book in some small way help the Moody ministries fulfill their goals.

I also want to acknowledge my parents and in-laws. I am as guilty as anyone for neglecting to express my appreciation to my parents for their sacrifice and patience. Thanks, Mom and Dad, and Eleanor and Bob, for pouring your lives into making mine (and Nancy's) so special.

In preparing this book, our company interviewed thousands of people about their attitudes, values, experiences, and expectations about family. I am grateful for each person who took the time to share his or her opinions and insights with us.

Last, but never least, is my own family. The research and reflection that went into this book has taught me much that will, I hope, enhance my future adventures with Nancy, my wife, and Samantha, my daughter. Both of them surrendered much while I was writing and researching this book. Nancy, I hope that what I'm striving to share with others will positively influence my own support for you as a friend, a husband, and a parent. Samantha, I pray that my absence from you while I was writing will in no way undermine our relationship or hinder your development as a young woman. Thank you both for your love, your support, your endurance, and your prayers.

Preface

Several years ago I was approached by a publisher who was familiar with my research and asked if I'd be interested in writing a book about the state of the family in America. But the overture to author a book on such a topic as broad as family did not fit in my vision of what I or my company do best. I needed to keep Barna Research focused, so I politely rejected the offer. At the time I figured that another book about family matters would simply get lost in the clutter of volumes already published on the subject.

Since then, I have led my company on a circuitous path to understand better what has happened to American culture in the past two decades and where America appears to be headed. In that process, one of my keenest interests has been to determine why so many millions of Americans find life these days to be frustrating and barely worth living. Many of our findings pointed to the breakdown of the family. Ironically, it was this same quest to understand the obstacles and means to a satisfying life that has led me to study family matters more deeply.

But why another book on families? Certainly others have written more persuasively and authoritatively on this subject. To my surprise, I found very little that offered a comprehensive, current, and reasonably unbiased perspective on the state of the American family. In addition, I recognized my company's ability to add new dimensions to the existing information base. I also became acutely aware of the tremendous biases within many of the "authoritative" works on family-related subjects. Don't misunderstand: I defend the right of individuals to state their point of view freely, whether it coincides with mine or not.

Nevertheless, the imbalance in how published works portray family matters surprised me. All too often, the literature regarding family embraces an underlying premise that the "traditional" notion of a family is antiquated, useless, or even harmful to society today. Indeed, much of what we see in media portrayals of families distorts past and present realities. Consider the prevailing views of family you are exposed to on a daily basis by the mass media:

- If you spend much time watching prime time television programs you would probably conclude that there are few married people left in America and that children from broken homes suffer no ill effects from that experience.
- Any viewer of the daily soap operas would have to assume that if he or she is not presently having an affair with someone else's spouse, then he or she must be the only one who is not engaging in such mischief—and ought to be ashamed for demonstrating such prudishness.
- Hollywood turns out movie after movie in which long-term, monogamous relationships are absent. Traditional families are depicted most often in an unfavorable or embarrassing light.
- Many print journalists write stories which assume that every family is struggling, that the number of homosexuals is growing rapidly, and that it is impossible for organizations or institutions to provide viable supports for the old-style family.
- Many media psychologists and talk show hosts, both radio and TV, give the impression that every family is dysfunctional and that your only hope for survival and true happiness is to take care of yourself at all costs.

Fortunately, those perspectives are quite simply wrong. The bottom line both in broadcast and print is that profits are generated through advertising and other fees, which are closely connected to the size of the audience they draw. Depiction of strong families is neither news nor entertaining. So the pictures we see and hear about usually represent an exception—ironically making the exception look like the norm.

In this book, I hope to provide a clear picture of the current state and likely future of the family in America. Granted, no communicator is capable of 100 percent objectivity. Every person enters the intensive study of a topic with assumptions, personal preferences, and a variety of expectations. I'm no different. So let me outline my own biases up front.

Personally, I believe that a traditional view of family makes the most sense and is the most beneficial for our culture. By "traditional," I mean people living together who are related to each other by marriage, birth, or adoption. This perspective is based on both my spiritual convictions (that is, that God created marriage and that children are a gift from God) and years of research on our culture, our values systems, the state of marriage and parenting, and other family-related matters. Having read many books, articles, reports, and other documents about family systems, philosophy of family, group dynamics, the psychology and sociology of family, and more, I have come to the conclusion that the Bible is the most insightful work ever written on family matters.

I fully recognize that our society is changing and that some of the forms of family that worked in the past do not work today. We must address these issues with reason and logic rather than emotion or selfishness. Of all the changes shaping families and people's lives today, which should we sanely defend and promote? Not every change is good for the American family.

I hope that my assessment of family conditions is fair and leads you to think more deeply about family issues. You are about to see, contrary to conventional wisdom, that the family in America is not dead. These findings reveal that the family will continue to face severe threats and challenges to what it could be, but is not in danger of being erased from our culture. I hope this information will help you face these pressures and challenges in your own family.

Note to the Reader

In this book, we make several references in surveys to "born-again Christians" and "evangelical Christians." Because there is considerable debate over what exactly these expressions mean, we believe it is important to provide readers with the definitions we use in Barna Research opinion polls.

Born-again Christians in this book refers to people who said in our surveys they have made a personal commitment to Jesus Christ that is still important in their lives today and who said that when they die they will go to heaven because they have confessed their sins and accepted Jesus Christ as their Savior. The Barna Research group classified these people as "born-again Christians" solely on the basis of their responses; whether people thought of themselves as born again or not was irrelevant to our research. In fact, at no point in our surveys were people given the opportunity to classify themselves as "born again" or as "born-again Christians."

Evangelical Christians refers to people who responded positively to essential beliefs that evangelical Christians hold in common. The responses required for such categorization were: belief that there is one all-powerful, all-knowing, perfect God who created the universe and rules it today; agreement with the born-again Christian criteria listed in the previous paragraph; a belief that religion is very important in their lives; agreement with the statement that the Bible is totally accurate in all that it teaches; a belief that they personally have a responsibility to share their religious beliefs with others who may think differently (and have so shared their religious beliefs in the past six months); rejection of the notion that all good people, whether they consider Christ to be their Savior or not, will live in heaven after they die on earth; and a willingness to classify themselves as Protestant, Catholic, or Christian.

CHAPTER ONE

THE CLEAVERS DON'T LIVE HERE ANYMORE

Turn on your television and watch a few reruns of programs popular in the late 1950s and early 1960s, such as "Ozzie and Harriet" or "Leave It to Beaver." Notice what the traditional family looked like (or was supposed to look like) in those days—the working father, the homemaker mother, and two school-age children. Listen to their conversations and think about the issues that concerned families in those days. Observe how parents interacted with each other and with their children and how they recognized the importance of family. As sanitized as they were, those old shows delivered a subtle yet powerful message: the family was an essential part of the American dream.

Not today. Open the daily newspaper or watch an evening newscast. What family-related issues or stories make the headlines? What do the families you see in the news or on television look like? For that matter, what is a family anymore? This last question is difficult to answer because "family" means all kinds of things to people today. The predictability and consistency that used to define the American family is long gone.

Americans are reeling from the changes that are reshaping their world. The past decade alone has witnessed radical technological advances, medical breakthroughs, challenges to our values system, a worldwide political realignment, and the advent of a global economy.

Some cultural analysts believe that our society now changes substantially in three-year cycles—a drastic acceleration of the ten or twenty-year cycles that used to mark significant transitions in our thinking and behavior.

People have reacted adversely to this lightning pace of change. Stress levels are going through the roof. Transience is widespread. Household finances are in disarray. People are blending pop psychology, orthodox Christianity, Eastern philosophy, and cultural truisms to create new worldviews. The doctor of choice for many families is no longer the general practitioner, but the psychologist.

FAMILIES ARE CHANGING

In times of rapid change, we desperately hold on to elements of our past because they provide us with a sense of stability and comfort. It is more of a reflex action than a conscious response. Even though most Americans do not really suppose, for instance, that the 1950s was a better decade to be alive, remembering the happy times and achievements of that era reassures and calms us as we face the uncertainty of the present.

Traditionally, one of the most important sources of stability has been our enduring faith in family. Despite the monumental social changes of recent times, we continue to maintain the belief that when all else fails, the family will be there to help pull us through. Regardless of whether that expectation is realistic or not, the peace of mind provided by such a notion still eases the anxiety of many Americans.

But will that bedrock of stability be there tomorrow? The past three decades have brought such fundamental change to our society that even the family has not escaped the strain. We can no longer assume that families offer stability, predictability, and dependability. Individuals are discovering—sometimes to their surprise and dismay—that coping effectively with life requires greater independence, personal strength, and purposefulness.

What is happening to the traditional family? In this book I provide specific data and analysis about recent changes that have undermined family values in America and what those changes will mean for the future of the family. This book is also a saga of Americans who struggle to sustain family relationships in the face of bewildering change. It lays out the hard facts to a nation that is slowly recognizing that stable family life has become the exception rather than the rule. Finally, I have written this book as a resource for Christians who want to protect cherished values from further erosion.

Regardless of their particular inclinations or beliefs, the vast majority of Americans care about the family.

Perhaps there is no better way to begin than to let some of the people we interviewed tell the story of the changing family, in their own words. Some articulate their position more eloquently than others. Some have clearly spent more time pondering today's circumstances than have others. Our research shows, though, that everyone has some pretty strong and definite feelings about the past, present, and future of the family in America.

The most impressive conclusion I've drawn from this research is that people believe that the health of our families is vitally important. Regardless of their particular inclinations or beliefs, the vast majority of Americans care about the family. And deep down in their hearts, they seem to know that as goes the family, so goes American society. The future of the family is not simply a matter of academic interest; it is an issue that touches directly on the well-being of American society itself.

Frances

Meet Frances Raymond. She is a schoolteacher in her early fifties. She has been married to the same man for more than half of her life. Together they have raised three children, all of whom are currently in college or living on their own. Although Frances has put in her time as a parent and teacher and remains around children all day long, she has not lost her sense of wonder about kids—nor her sense of fear about the world they will inherit.

"When I was young, I used to dream about getting married, having children—I thought five or six would be ideal, just like my mother, until I had a few of my own—and living in the same house from the time we were married until we retired, or maybe even until we died. Family was such an ideal back then. It was expected of you, but it was also the most pleasant lifestyle we could imagine.

"Things have changed, of course. Today, I'm the odd woman out at school, the only one on my entire floor who has remained married to—or at least faithful to—the same man for any period of time. I know they snicker at me behind my back sometimes because they think I'm old-fashioned. It's so unbelievable, really.

"Think about what these kids today are going to contend with when they are old enough to get married. Will people even marry then? I don't know. Somewhere along the line we got off track and never got back on it. And I'm convinced we're worse off for that. And it's today's young ones who will suffer the most for that diversion."

Paul

Younger adults may lack Frances's sense of history, but many of them voice her concern about the direction of the family these days. Paul Robertson is typical of this perspective. In his late twenties, born at the tail end of the Baby Boom, he is an aggressive, achievement-oriented marketing professional. College-educated and single, he expresses the worries of many of his peers.

"I want to get married, but it's a scary proposition. I can't think of anyone I know who either hasn't been through a divorce, or is happy in their marriage. My own parents split when I was still in junior high. It killed me. It killed my brothers and sister, too. Yeah, divorce isn't inevitable, but man, it sure seems like everyone struggles with marriage.

"I'm sure I'll find the right person eventually, but I just hope I'm not too old, or too paranoid about a failed marriage to miss my chance. I want to have kids, too. Little kids are great. I just don't buy that line about how it's not fair to bring kids into a rotten world like this. It is a rotten world, but I got through it okay, my friends made their way through it, and my kids can, too. But I've got a long way to go before having children is a real concern for me. Relationships are tough these days."

Bill

Even those who have a professional responsibility to assist the family are often baffled by the conditions they face. Psychologists, priests, ministers, counselors, and lawyers express widespread confusion about what is happening, why it is happening, and what the most appropriate responses are to the vast changes that are reshaping the American family. Reverend Bill Hellix describes his frustrations.

"How do you counsel an engaged couple anymore? I can't tell them that marriage will be one giant pleasure ride because it's not true and nobody would buy that line. I don't want to scare them off with some of the horror stories I've seen in my past counseling with couples who never should have been married to start with. Living together is not a viable option, based on the beliefs that I hold, so I can't encourage that route.

"By training, I know I'm supposed to turn to the Bible and say 'Everything you need to know about love and having a successful family life is right here.' But hey, I wasn't born yesterday. I know most of them would sit there with that pleasant grin on their faces and think 'Okay, we'll tolerate this bozo and his arcane advice because we need someone to legally marry us.'

"So I talk with them about some of the scenarios they might encounter and offer the best advice I can. Maybe that will better prepare them for the rough waters that it seems every family faces these days. I'll tell you, I don't care who you are and how strong your faith is, having a real family in this age is no picnic.

"So after a lot of soul searching and agonizing I've concluded that maybe I can help the most by letting couples know that when they encounter trouble—and they will—there are alternatives to divorce, that they're not the first couple to go through the wringer, and that I'll do my best to stand with them through the storm. I encourage them to seek God's guidance, but to most young people today, that type of advice is from another era. They see it as religious talk that has no real meaning. Sometimes, no, usually, I feel like I'm out of my element, even though I know that what I'm saying is right and true."

SURPRISING FACTS ABOUT THE FAMILY

In the Age of Information, what can be told about the family that hasn't already been a "Factoid" on CNN, a "Snapshot" in *USA Today,* or a nugget for comment by the likes of Paul Harvey? Geraldo, Phil, and Oprah attract sizable audiences because they feature the offbeat family as entertainment. In their discussions of the contemporary family, they consistently ignore content, stable homes and focus instead on the aberrant, the bizarre, and the outrageous.

In the chapters that follow, we will trace a different picture of the family in America today than is presented by the major media and the politically correct analysts of our era. Undeniably, family is different today than it was a quarter-century ago, yet it continues to thrive. Even so-called old-fashioned values show a real staying power. Consider, for instance, these surprising facts about the family in America in the mid-nineties.

- Marriage is not dead. Nine out of ten Americans still get to wear a wedding band at some point in their lives. (See chapter 3.)
- Cohabitation may be a seemingly sensible step prior to marriage, but it is not a viable protection against divorce. People who live together before marriage actually have a substantially higher likelihood of getting divorced than do those who live separately prior to voicing their vows. (Cohabitation is addressed in chapter 6.)
- Parents do not credit themselves with having the greatest impact on their own children. But they do not charge the media with that influence, either. They cite their kids' friends as the biggest influencers. (Read about parents and

children in chapter 5.)

■ Politicians and journalists generally claim that 10 percent of all American adults are practicing homosexuals. The truth is that homosexuals represent about 1 percent of the population—a vocal, powerful, but numerically minuscule segment. (Homosexuals and family life as they see it are discussed in chapter 7.)

■ Before they reach the age of eighteen, two out of three children born this year will live in a single-parent household. (Chapter 4 provides further insights about divorce and single-parent households.)

■ Single-parent households are becoming more common in America. Sadly, the majority of those families live in, or on the verge of, poverty. (This situation is described in chapter 4.)

■ More than half of all mothers with children under six years of age are currently in the labor force. (Chapter 9 has details.)

■ Religion is a matter of increasing curiosity and concern among Americans. However, traditional faiths have less influence on people's family life than many individuals might suppose. (This topic is explored in depth in chapter 10.)

■ One of the emerging trends is for single adults who are in their twenties and thirties to opt for returning home to live with their parents. (Consult chapter 6 for further information.)

■ Having your first child? Chances are almost fifty-fifty that you will not be married to the child's other parent. (See chapter 5.)

■ Family values and lifestyles differ significantly between whites, blacks, and Hispanics. (Racial and ethnic distinctions are examined in chapter 8.)

■ Contrary to popular belief, most homemakers are even more satisfied with the quality of their lives than are women who have children and work outside the home. (This is noted in chapter 3.)

There is ample evidence that the family is in the midst of a fundamental transition. The coming decade promises to bring even more sweeping changes in the way we think about the family. Those transitions will, of course, have a substantial impact on the future of our nation, the strength of our religious institutions, and our fulfillment as individuals.

It's true: the Cleavers don't live here anymore. The close, extended families, the pristine, safe neighborhoods, stable jobs, and peaceful homes of earlier days have almost disappeared from American life. But there is cause for hope. Despite the hostile forces arrayed against it, the traditional family can make a comeback. And this book will help you and your church take the first step toward that goal by understanding specifically how American families have held up under the stress of recent times. What better time could there be than today to explore the dimensions of these changes and to consider how we might influence the outcome?

CHAPTER TWO

THE NOUVEAU FAMILY

A couple sits down to dinner with their two children. They discuss the day's events as the food is passed around. School and work dominate the conversation. The children complain about having to eat their vegetables. Over dessert, they make plans to take a bike trip to a nearby town. They clear the table together quickly to watch a television special. A typical family, right? Except that we've left out one important piece of information: the two adults are both women. They are lovers who have made a commitment to live together. The children are from previous marriages. Now would you describe this group as a family?

The answer you hear to this question today depends largely on the person you ask. More and more Americans are broadening the customary definitions of family to include people not related by blood or marriage: lovers of the same or opposite sex, groups that share a common interest, and even casual acquaintances are but a few examples. Such arrangements are often called nouveau families.

Are nouveau families just a fad, or are they here to stay? Are they an isolated development, or are they an indicator of a major shift in the character of the American family? Before we examine the implications of this development, we should look more closely at the characteristics of both traditional and nouveau families.

TRADITIONAL AND NOUVEAU FAMILIES

Recent public opinion surveys have discovered that people still believe in the worth of the traditional family. But what exactly is a "traditional" family? Generally speaking, it refers to people who are related to each other by marriage, birth, or adoption. The married couple without children, the married couple with children, parents and their adopted or natural children, and extended families (grandparents, parents, children, aunts, uncles, nephews, cousins) could all fit into such a category. (Throughout this book, I will rely on this definition when discussing the traditional family.) These days, when people are asked to define "family," about half of them (46 percent in our most recent study) offer descriptions that most researchers would call traditional.

But a significant shift has occurred in people's thinking over the last twenty years. Most Americans feel that describing family simply in terms of married people, their children, and perhaps their close relatives (such as grandparents, cousins, aunts, and uncles) is too restrictive and old-fashioned. In fact, two-thirds of all adults describe their families in ways that can be called to some degree nouveau or alternative. Moreover, nearly half of all adults have some notion of family that draws on both traditional and nouveau ideas. In other words, adults whose definition of family can be called traditional for the most part have also embraced some alternative descriptions of family. (See Table 2.1 for additional details.)

Essentially, the nouveau family can be defined as two or more people who care about each other. The individuals need not be related by marriage or other legal bonds, nor even be living together. What must be true of them, instead, is that they demonstrate, either tangibly or intangibly, a significant degree of mutual care or concern. Because this definition includes no requirements or assumptions of permanence, the boundaries of family are fluid. The common experience that traditional and nouveau families share is that of close emotional ties or special bonds between people. For some, this means marriage or children; for others, it means any relationship in which people care about or intimately relate to each other. In the minds of Americans, the essence of family is a shared experience or emotion.

People's views of family are closely related to their present circumstances and cultural upbringing. Adults who have never been married, for instance, are unlikely to describe a family as consisting of married adults, regardless of whether children are present in the home. Baby Busters (that group of people born between 1965 and 1983), who have been exposed to alternative families more than any prior generation, are more likely than older Americans to express nontraditional ideas in describing their families. Today's young people, like the generations that went before them, clearly reflect the environmental conditioning of their time.

Speaking with young adults reveals how deeply the nouveau way of thinking has taken hold. One respondent said, "My family is all the people who I really care about, and who really care about me. Family means that there is a relationship between us in which the most important thing is that we take care of each other, at least emotionally, if not physically." Another Baby Buster put it this way: "My family is actually my circle of close friends, the people who know me and accept me and look out for me." Some young people have created even broader definitions. "To me, family is more than just my parents and brothers. It's all the people I'm comfortable with, the ones I get along with." A woman in her mid-thirties described her view of family as "the people you can count on when needed. For me, that means my real friends. When I'm down or in trouble, they're the ones I turn to for strength. That's the real meaning of family." (Table 2.1 reveals how family is defined according to age group.)

Some definitions of nouveau family sound remarkably similar to those of traditional families. "It's all the people with whom you have long-term, close ties or relationships"; "people who live together and share their lives with each other"; "the group of people who love and protect each other." But those offering these definitions frequently go on to reveal that marriage, adoption, or birth do not necessarily have to be included in this view of family. "Well, that's really the old way of thinking," lectured one male from the upper Midwest who is in his late thirties and is married with two children. "It's not the legal bonds that are so important; what really counts is the emotional strings that weave people together. I can show you many homes with a husband and wife and kids who really are so disconnected from each other that they can't possibly be thought of as a family. And I can introduce you to my closest and dearest friends, who must be considered part of my true family. They are the ones who make my life worth living."

The Roper Organization, a respected research firm, conducted its own nationwide survey on families recently. (See Table 2.2 for a more extensive description of their results.) That study confirmed that Americans consider almost any combination of heterosexual people involved in some kind of personal relationship to be a family. The majority of Americans refuse to include homosexual couples in this category, however. Still, even one out of every four adults is willing to grant gay couples family status, and the expectation is that this percentage will increase in the coming years.

The Roper statistics also highlight two other insights. First, to Americans almost any household with children constitutes a family, regardless of the number or gender of adults present. Indeed, to millions of Americans, family is about children. When kids are not present, most people will acknowledge some kind of relationship between consenting adults but may or may not consider the couple to be a family.

A second finding is that households with single-parent mothers are more likely to be characterized as families than are homes headed by a single-parent father. Women are more easily identified with family than men, even if all their circumstances are otherwise similar.

WHY THE SHIFT?
In more cases than not, people have come to embrace a more inclusive definition of family because they believe the traditional family configurations have failed them personally. Either they have experienced a

TABLE 2.1 How Americans Define Family

		Percentage holding traditional view	Percentage holding nouveau view
👫	Married	47%	69%
👤	Single	43%	67%
👫	Divorced	46%	69%
👤	Widowed	50%	64%
18–27		37%	75%
28–46		47%	66%
47–64		48%	71%
65 and older		52%	60%
All		46%	68%

Source: "Family in America" survey conducted in February 1992 by the Barna Research Group, Ltd. These data reflect the answers of 1,009 people interviewed in the study. Percentages exceed 100 percent because some respondents gave answers that fit both "traditional" and "nouveau" categories.

divorce (as a marriage partner or as a child born to the divorced parents), are putting up with a bad marriage, or have endured some other type of stressful family conditions. But having been raised with the notion that "family is good," most Americans are reluctant to reject wholly the idea of family. In typical American fashion, we instead attempt to innovate, creating a new understanding or model that will serve us better in changing times. Many adults have modified traditional standards so as to improve their chances of having a "successful" family, one on which they can rely in times of need.

The Effects of the Industrial Revolution

An even more important force in reshaping attitudes has been the social, economic, and cultural changes of the past century. In particular, the industrial age, which began in the nineteenth century, continued to expand and transform American life in the twentieth century. Increasingly, family incomes and lifestyles were influenced by new developments in machinery and manufacturing. Economic pressures and opportunities often broke apart extended families or forced them to adapt to new circumstances.

One important change was the separation of the workplace from the home. In an agricultural economy, families usually worked and lived off the same plot of land. The family labored together to produce a crop for its own needs or to sell to a larger market. By contrast, in a manufacturing-oriented economy, labor was performed in urban areas and in large, impersonal factories. The lure of higher pay and the declining prices for agricultural products drew many rural families to the cities. The partnership of people laboring together, day in and day out, to accomplish common tasks for the good of the group, disintegrated.

But the spread of factories did more than just reshape the economy. The industrial age created an entirely new view of life. Millions believed the promise that "progress" could improve living standards. The industrial age was responsible for expanding interpersonal relationships, opening up new jobs and occupational training, creating higher wages and increased disposable income, boosting life expectancy, introducing public education, modifying sex roles, expanding leisure time, and redirecting the economic ambitions of families.

TABLE 2.2 Living Arrangements Considered to Be Families

Living Arrangement	Is this a family? Yes	No
Married couple living with their children	98%	1%
Married couple living with their children from a previous marriage	93%	5%
A man and woman who are married but do not have any children	87%	10%
A divorced mother living with her children	84%	13%
An unwed, never-married mother living with her children	81%	14%
A divorced father living with his children	80%	17%
A man and woman who live together for a long time but are not married, but are raising children together	77%	17%
An unwed, never-married father living with his children	73%	19%
A man and woman who live together for a long time but are not married	53%	37%
A group of unrelated adults who live together and consider themselves a family	28%	60%
Two lesbian women living with children that they are raising	27%	62%
Two gay men living with children that they are raising	26%	65%
Two lesbian women committed to each other and who are living together	21%	69%
Two gay men committed to each other and who are living together	20%	71%

Source: Survey conducted in February 1992 by the Roper Organization and published in *The Public Perspective* 3, no. 5 (July-August 1992):101. These data reflect the answers of 1,000 people interviewed in the study. Percentages do not add up to 100 percent due to respondents who gave "don't know" replies.

Long before the sexual revolution of the 1960s, the age of industrialization created the first major shift in male-female roles. Until this time, the man of the house usually worked in the fields adjacent to his home and was involved in the day-to-day care of the family. His wife attended to childrearing and tasks in the home, and together they formed an integrated partnership, blending their time and talents. Upon accepting a job at a factory, however, a man could seldom remain close to his home and often left his wife home alone with the family for most of the day. It was at this point in history that the woman assumed the role of isolated housewife and mother while the father typically worked off-premises as a hired hand in someone else's business.

This separation of home and workplace had other consequences. Public schools assumed greater responsibility for education and also became responsible for transmitting values and socializing children. As the numbers of farm families decreased, children were seldom needed to labor in the fields. The necessity of forcing young people to mature quickly and assume adult responsibilities at younger ages also vanished. Laws were passed to protect children from having to do the work that just a few decades earlier might have been required for the very survival of their families. Other laws prohibiting child abuse and providing for a public-funded education were also instituted.

Technological breakthroughs affected the family profoundly. The automobile, for instance, changed dating and courting practices and expanded employment options. New methods of communication and entertainment allowed people to escape the confinement of urban areas. The telephone, for example, lessened the need for face-to-face communication and often increased isolation and privacy. Movies not only entertained but passed on important cultural trends. Central heating in homes meant that people no longer had to share the same room (the "family room") for free-time activities. Electricity appeared in most homes, and the labor-saving devices that used this power freed up time and enabled people to enjoy leisure interests. Public education was opened up for women, enabling more females to take on full-time jobs.

The cumulative effect of all these changes was to weaken loyalties and attachments to the family. Up to this time, the family was usually the strongest influence in a person's life. Not only did it look out for the interests of each member, but it contributed collectively to the welfare of a wider community. Industrialization, fragmenting people's lives as it did, dissolved this sense of obligation and encouraged individuals to look after their own interests. The family has yet to recover from that shift.

The Effects of the Sexual Revolution

There was yet another development that affected the traditional family significantly. Beginning in the 1960s, traditional sexual and cultural attitudes in America came under fire. Birth control, child care, sexual equality, working women, "no fault" divorce, legalized abortion, interracial marriages, and unwed mothers became commonplace. The traditional family found itself competing with strange ideas and practices that were passed off as acceptable alternatives to father-mother-child relationships, including homosexual families, multiple partner arrangements, and communes. The effects of these changes remain with us today and show no signs of weakening.

One of the greatest effects of the sexual revolution has been to make the nouveau family respectable in many people's eyes. Supporters of alternative families, who claim that they have much in common with those who belong to traditional families, are gaining a hearing. They maintain that they are seeking the support and nurture that traditional families offer, only in a different setting with different partners. They also insist that they want to reap the benefits of family–life maintenance (that is, the provision of physical and emotional support), socialization, sexual intimacy, reproduction, and social status—without confining legal or social restrictions. As we shall see, however, the implications of this viewpoint are troubling.

A Breakdown in Thinking About Truth

The breakdown in sexual morality that occurred in the 1960s was the consequence of a more serious breakdown in thinking about the truth. The biblical view of truth posits that the ultimate authority in all matters of life, including family, is a matter of absolutes, not a matter of choices.

Truth is not one of several alternatives one might or might not embrace according to one's personal preference. For many years this thinking about truth was reflected in the moral standards considered generally acceptable throughout the country and in legislation proposed and enacted. But over time, a pluralistic view took over. It posited that the ultimate authority was self, mediated by society and its laws. Whereas religious beliefs may inform some of the family-based decisions people make, neither the Bible nor any other religious-based teaching is considered inerrant.

Once this position concerning truth took over, it was probably inevitable that it would impact our thinking about the family. The issue of choice, which we usually associate with the question of abortion, can be applied just as well to those who demand recognition and protection for all nontraditional forms of family. Personal freedom, people argue, has been suffocated by the restrictions and rules that society has imposed on families. By abolishing those rules and allowing people to make uninhibited choices, an individual can create the kind of family best suited to his or her needs. Our research has revealed that this philosophy is reflected in current lifestyles and attitudes.

In family matters, this underlying difference over the nature of truth shows itself in the battle lines drawn between conservatives and liberals. On one side are conservatives, who believe that the choice of what is right and wrong has already been made for humankind by God. On the other are liberals, who believe that morality is a personal matter and can only be defined according to each individual's needs and best interests.

Because the conservative perspective stems from Judeo-Christian beliefs in which personal morality is judged according to absolute standards set forth in Scripture, people who embrace this view will see certain behavior as always wrong, no matter how much society condones the activity. The liberal viewpoint, in contrast, which maintains that morality is relative and that the Bible and other religious-based teaching are neither inerrant nor authoritative, will see personal choice as the key to fulfillment in life and will work for a relaxation of traditional standards of family life and sexuality. Liberals believe that only the individual can make proper decisions about what is best for himself. Consequently, when humankind has been effectively liberated from a "Victorian" (in other words, restrictive, paranoid, unrealistic, and inhumane) view of male-female roles and family obligations, then true "freedom" and fulfillment can be realized. The nineties are thus seen as an era in which people cast off unwarranted stigmas, restrictive relationships, and sexual limitations.

WHAT THE NOUVEAU FAMILY MEANS FOR AMERICANS

The rising acceptance of the nouveau view of family has some important—and frightening—implications for our society. First, it suggests that family is not a permanent relationship. At any time, as soon as one of the people involved in the "family" feels that he or she is either not adequately being cared for or feels drawn to other individuals, the definition of that person's family instantly changes. Our research discovered that this possibility is actually attractive to some adults. "The reality of family is that it is a group of people who understand and meet my needs," was how one forty-seven-year-old man put it. "When the people I'm living or interacting with cease to really know me or to truly care for me, that's when I have to rethink my relationships and recreate a family that works for my needs."

Yet those who advocate such loose family ties often fail to grasp that successful families are successful largely because they offer safety, trust, and permanence. Once a family ceases to offer those protections, the atmosphere for love and intimacy is lost. Opportunities for personal and joint growth are largely forfeited. Ultimately, the family falters because its members refuse to surrender some of their freedoms for the benefit of others.

Second, the nouveau definition dilutes the distinctive character of the family. Ultimately, any person or group of people may be deemed family. Family becomes synonymous with friendship. Street gangs become a family. A softball team that plays together after work becomes a family. A neighborhood watch group, created to protect each other, becomes a family. The people you enjoy hanging out with at lunchtime are a family. Even people who may never have met each other but who possess an intense, common desire to protect the whales can be deemed a family.

Although some people may find this view open-minded and emotionally appealing, they must also face up to the fact that "family" will cease to have any fixed meaning. For some people, family becomes no more than a series of acquaintances and transient connections.

Third, the nouveau definition legitimizes such a broad array of relationships that the inevitable result is the disintegration of trust in the permanence and reliability of love. Love, in fact, is made to mean whatever the individuals involved say it is. For instance, in the nouveau family, a unit composed of a married adult and a lover (of the same or opposite gender) qualifies as a family. Thus, each individual may have a variety of sexual relationships, all of which qualify as "family" relationships and are justifiable according to this uninhibited point of view. The logical progression of the nouveau philosophy would be to remove the barriers to aberrant lifestyles, such as polygamy, bisexual relations, and group sex.

Fourth, the nouveau perspective undermines many of the legal protections now afforded to the traditional family. If our laws are revised to extend rights to nouveau families, as appears likely, the effects will be far-reaching. Those pushing alternative family agendas will gain greater access to government services, increased legal rights, and wider influence in the media and schools.

When it is clearly and narrowly defined, the family retains its strength and influence.

The history of America demonstrates that our perspectives on the family often change in response to new cultural conditions and thinking. Usually a perspective at a given moment in time is conditioned by the lifestyles and values currently in vogue, media portrayals of family life, the dominant philosophies about human relationships, the depth of commitment to a religious-based perspective on family, and the influence of government policies and regulations regarding families. As we enter the mid-nineties, the most popular view of family is inclining away from traditional values.

Lasting, stable families are possible, however, only if society is willing to restrict its definition of family in order to combat threats to its existence. Despite the willingness of government statisticians and social scientists to accept nouveau ideas and definitions of family, we must keep in mind that these groups are merely responding to the ways in which people think and behave. As long as the American people tolerate the equal status of alternative family arrangements, they can expect only increasing confusion and discord in their personal relationships. When an entity becomes so broad that it includes everything, it generally ceases to have significance. This is particularly true of the family. When it is clearly and narrowly defined, the family retains its strength and influence.

Though freedom is a cherished value in America , it can also undermine our society if pursued without restraint. Once individuals refuse to acknowledge that freedom must go hand in hand with individual responsibility and consideration for others, it is very difficult to convince them that the undisciplined exercise of such freedom is not in their best interests. Because of human arrogance, we tend to believe we can master any situation and make it work for our good, regardless of how it affects others.

Our research indicates that America will not likely embrace a more conservative or biblical view of family matters in the coming decade. To ignite such a reversal of thought and behavior would take strong, compelling leadership at multiple levels: national, state, community, and family. In fact, given the pervasiveness of nontraditional ideas, we may see in the 1990s more laws and court decisions that uphold nouveau family arrangements. We might also expect growing indifference to how families are defined. And we are likely to witness a decade in which millions of Americans suffer the consequences of family relationships in which freedom outweighs responsibility, self-centered need overpowers mutual trust, and the reigning cultural values replace traditional, Bible-based perspectives.

HOW CHRISTIANS CAN RESPOND

For individuals who believe that God cares about our families and wants us to follow His ways, the nineties will be a time of both battle and opportunity.

The battle will be to redefine the family in a sensible manner. We must insist that the standards set forth in God's Word become the basis for family policies, systems, and teaching. From a biblical perspective, the casual way in which Americans regard their families is unnecessary, harmful, and at its root, sinful.

We need to develop constructive ways of making influential people in our country—politicians, media executives, writers, artists, musicians, educators, business executives, and religious leaders—aware that there is a huge contingent of adults who remain committed to God's design for the family. The nineties will provide us with many opportunities to speak with people about the importance of family-related issues.

We need also to examine our own lives to see if we are conforming in any way to nouveau family concepts. If we are tolerating situations that clearly contradict God's Word, we must turn from those circumstances and recommit ourselves to families that are grounded in biblically based principles.

Most Americans are searching for reasonable answers to the hard questions raised by our daily experience. If a neighbor came to you with such questions, would you be prepared to offer a sensible argument for the traditional family? By studying God's Word and thinking through the implications of today's lifestyles, you will be ready when presented with the opportunity to discuss your values with those who are lost and hurting or with those who reject traditional values.[1]

Notes

1. The Bible is packed with teaching, stories, and practical applications regarding the family. In particular, I found the following passages to be helpful: Genesis 1–2; Deuteronomy 6:1–9; Proverbs 3:11–12, 6:20–23, 13:24, 22:6, 22:15, 23:13–14, 29:15; Matthew 12:46–50, 15:21–28, 18:1–10, 19:1–15; 1 Corinthians 7; Ephesians 5:22–29, 6:14; 1 Thessalonians 2:7–12; and 1 Timothy 5:3–16. You might want to investigate the Bible yourself to find additional family-related topics. It would also be useful to read what other Christian leaders have written about the family. Some useful insights can be drawn from the work of James Dobson, Chuck Swindoll, John MacArthur, Kevin Leman, Norman Wright, Gary Trent and John Smalley, and Merton Strommen.

CHAPTER THREE

MARRIAGE IS ALIVE AND WELL

$$S$$ally Winfield. It used to be Sally Alston. "I did it just right," she exclaims playfully. "When I was young, my last name began with "A," so I'd always get to go first, be at the front of the line. Now, when I'm older and more tired and don't want to go first, I'm at the back of the line with the W's."

But Sally is hardly old. She's in her mid-thirties and generally gets a kick out of life. She married Tom Winfield a year after graduating from college, where they had met and dated for a couple of years. He's an engineer; she works part-time as a customer relations specialist for a computer software firm. She scaled back her hours when the first of their two children was born. She places both children, ages two and five, in a child care program a block from her job.

Marriage was always something that Sally assumed would happen in her life. "When I was young, the girls in the neighborhood used to come over to my house and we'd talk about our future lives in great detail. We'd talk about the color of the house we'd live in, what type of furniture we'd buy, how many children we'd have, the types of cars we'd own, and what our husbands would do for a living." She pauses to reflect for a moment, then continues with a laugh. "Not one of my predictions has come true.

"Actually, though, marriage has been good. It has some tough moments, but then what relationship doesn't? Tom's a good balance for me. I'm aggressive, energetic, kind of wild sometimes. Tom, bless his heart, calls it 'spirited.' He's the typical engineer: very steady, pensive, level-headed. Not a nerd, but a deeper thinker, soft-spoken, the let's-wait-and-see type. It took us a while to figure out how to make this marriage work, but I think we've pretty much got it covered now."

Having recently moved into an area "infested with kids," she notes that most of her contact is now with other married adults. She perceives that most people have the wrong expectations when it comes to marriage. "A lot of today's adults think that marriage just happens, that it is a relationship that will magically iron itself out. No way. I can't think of anything I've done in life that has put me through more stress, more pressure, more anxiety, more emotional distress than our marriage. It takes a lot of time and a lot of care, because if you don't make it a priority, it's bound to fall apart. I think the reason most marriages fail is because the people didn't realize how tough it'd be, and didn't have a serious commitment to make it last."

Upon reflection, she realizes that marriage and male-female relationships aren't discussed much at work. "You watch the reruns on cable of the old shows, like 'Leave It to Beaver' and 'Father Knows Best,' and family stuff was always a hot topic of conversation. But now that you mention it, I can't recall the last time we sat down for lunch or at a break and discussed family stuff. We talk about all kinds of things—politics, religion, housing, the cost of living, health issues—but family never seems to emerge. Except, of course, when there's some madman who wipes out an entire family with a machete. Then, we talk about crime, weapon control, and the grief the family must be experiencing."

When she thinks about the future of marriage, she admits to being a bit perplexed. "People certainly are trying everything else imaginable, aren't they? But I can't imagine how else we're going to make sense of life, aside from marriage and family and some of the traditional approaches to life." She pauses to laugh at her own remark, recognizing the irony of her statement. "Who would have thought that Sally Winfield would ever have promoted anything remotely related to a traditional lifestyle? In college, I'm the one who organized the boycotts and rallied students to protest the traditional core curriculum and traditional testing practices. I designed our wedding ceremony so that it wouldn't be a traditional, stale, and staid wedding. None of those standard vows for me! And here I am, standing up for the traditional family in America. Strange world, isn't it?"

Many media and social analysts, citing a wealth of emotionally riveting but unrepresentative case histories, are declaring that the traditional marriage is on its last legs. This warning is nothing new. So-called experts have been proclaiming the imminent death of marriage since the late sixties. However, the intensity with which these experts have made the assertion and the degree to which the public has accepted this claim have both increased considerably in the past decade.

Not that there isn't sufficient reason to question the vitality of marriage in present-day America. Just look at some of the statistics that support the marriage-is-dead argument. In 1970, 71 percent of all adults were part of a married-couple family. The same arrangement had plummeted to just 55 percent by 1991.[1] There is little reason to believe that the trend will be reversed in the coming years. In fact, some demographers are confidently predicting that a majority of American adults will be single by the time we usher in the twenty-first century.

The dramatic rise in divorce has definitely shaken Americans' confidence in marriage. Young adults in particular harbor significant doubts. In survey after survey people under thirty express more skepticism about the viability of marriage than do older individuals. Most adults under thirty (75 percent) believe that it is either hard or impossible to have a good marriage these days. In part, this is due to their feeling that few of the married people they know have an ideal relationship. And, argue today's young adults, what good is marriage if it isn't ideal?[2]

OBSERVING OUR PARENTS

Part of the struggle that young adults have with the image of marriage relates to the couple they have observed first-hand. Most Americans' views on marriage have been profoundly colored, for better or worse, by their personal experiences with their parents. Because we learn best by observing behavior that has been modeled for us, many Americans who are now in their teens or twenties assume that the marital struggles they watched during their formative years are the norm for all marriages.

Having observed troubled marriages, many young adults have been frightened by the prospect of having to endure that kind of hardship and tension in their own lives. "I watched these two grown people, people whom I loved and wanted to be like, fight like cats and dogs for twenty-some years. They'd fight about big things and small things, it didn't matter," recalled a young single adult from the Midwest. "As I got older, I remember thinking to myself, 'These are the people I love. And these are the people I'm supposed to be like? Forget it.' I figured that if this was their idea of fun, I'd forgo that kind of fun in my own life. If that's as good as it gets, I don't need it."

Most adults say that they love their parents and appreciate the efforts they made toward establishing a stable home life. Yet it is a minority of young adults (45 percent) who say they would like to have a marriage like that of their parents.[3] It is little wonder that so many young people are dubious about the long-term potential of any marriage.

Skepticism about marriage and fidelity is widespread today.

The examples of turbulent marriages and the fear of failure are so strong in our culture that even when things are satisfying in one's own marriage, there remains significant anxiety about the general state of the institution. As treasured as marriage seems to be in our culture, it is widely thought to be doomed because its track record seems to confirm its inherent weakness. One national study discovered that nine out of ten married people claim that they have been faithful to their spouses but that only one out of four adults believes that other married couples display the same degree of fidelity.[4]

The assumption that one's own marriage is secure but that marriage in general is not likely to endure is a phenomenon that sociologist Andrew Greeley calls "pluralistic ignorance." One of our survey respondents, a man in his early forties, voiced such ideas. "I really can't see myself renting a hotel room, or creeping in the shadows to some other place, to have an affair." He lives in the Northeast and was well aware that such behavior was common in his region. "I know I'm living in the Dark Ages, morally, compared to my peers. I'm probably the only person left in my area who hasn't gotten it on with another woman, behind my wife's back. Frankly, I don't hold much hope for marriage, in the long run. Doris and I will make it okay, but I'm sure we'll be the exception to the rule."

Skepticism about marriage and fidelity is widespread today. And certainly the numerous incidents of adultery that occur each day suggest that there is reason to question Americans' commitment to marriage. Nevertheless, when we look harder at the statistics, we realize that marriage in America is still thriving. Divorce, cohabitation, and the large proportion of single adults notwithstanding, *nine out of ten Americans get married.*[5] Most American adults are currently married. Most divorced people get remarried. Most people who cohabit do so as preparation for their intended marriage. The vast majority of married people describe their union as "very happy."[6] Married adults, overall, are so satisfied with their mates that 89 percent say that if they had a second chance, they would marry the same person.[7] And among all adults who have never been wed, more than four out of five (84 percent) say they would like to get married someday.[8] Marriage may take a beating from the critics, who cite numerous examples of failed unions. However, marriage appears to remain a popular, desirable, and potentially fulfilling alternative to remaining single.

A minister of a Presbyterian church expressed his amazement at this reality. "After I graduated from seminary, I assumed that I'd spend more time counseling people for divorces and preparing words of consolation for families of those who had died than I would engaging people in conversation about an impending marriage. I've been astounded at how many people still want to get married—and how many follow through on that desire. If marriage is dying, somebody should tell the people in this area about it, because they still seem to think that marriage is the thing to do."

Increasingly, support for traditional family systems is coming from unexpected sources.

This church leader then described other surprises he has encountered in talking to people about marriage. He senses a widespread belief that marriage will occur less frequently in our culture. Still, the people he counsels do not wish to avoid or escape marriage personally. They share their hope that the institution will survive and be strengthened.

ATTITUDES ABOUT MARRIAGE

Marriage may be thousands of years old, but fewer than one out of every ten adults contends that it is an outdated idea that no longer fits our nation's culture.[9] This is a significant finding because it seems to fly in the face of the popular notion that the nineties will be a time when individuals will discard marriage in favor of other living arrangements. At a time when traditional institutions of all kinds—social, political, and economic—are being toppled, it is of no small importance that people continue to cling to marriage.

In fact, a large majority of people concur that marriage is critical for the health of our country. Seven out of ten adults state that "if the traditional family unit falls apart, the stability of American society will collapse." These are strong, surprisingly conservative sentiments coming from a society that prides itself for having open minds to progressive ideas.[10]

Increasingly, support for traditional family systems is coming from unexpected sources. After years of tolerating and even encouraging alternative family forms, many counselors, medical doctors, and ministers from mainline churches are concluding that marriage and stable families are critical to healthy personal development and to the well-being of our society.

One expert who has taken such a stand is Dr. Armand Nicholi, a respected professor at the Harvard Medical School and a staff physician at Massachusetts General Hospital. Dr. Nicholi recently encouraged an audience of young adults to seriously consider the value derived from a healthy family system.

"Why talk about family? We all fall short and the talk only makes us uncomfortable. The answer is simple. Our family experience is the most significant experience of our lives. No human interaction has greater impact on our lives than our family experience. . . .

"The breakdown of the family contributes significantly to the major problems confronting our society today. Research data make unmistakably clear a strong relationship between broken families and the drug epidemic, the increase in out-of-wedlock pregnancies, the rise in violent crime, and the unprecedented epidemic of suicide among children and adolescents. . . .

"We need a radical change in our thinking about family. We need a society where people have the freedom to be whatever they choose—but if they choose to have children, then those children must be given the highest priority."[11]

The outlook people have on the long-term endurance of marriages is no less surprising—or traditional. Perhaps it is our nation's Christian heritage, or perhaps our near-neurotic fear of failure, that leads most people to believe that a marriage is meant to be a lifelong relationship and should never be ended except under extreme circumstances. Even the under-thirty-five group—younger adults who typically have the least supportive views of traditional values and lifestyles—agree that marriage is not supposed to be a here-today-gone-tomorrow experience. As one twenty-four-year-old unmarried woman who is engaged for the second time put it, "Who wants to look failure in the eye each morning when you turn over in bed? If I'm gonna surrender my sexual freedom and voluntarily put restraints on how I can spend my time, I'm gonna make . . . sure that this is the right guy. If for no other reason, it's in my best interests to minimize my own pain; the more marriages you have, the more painful and humiliating it's got to be."

In fact, 79 percent of adults of all ages contend that "God intended for people to get married and stay in that relationship for life."[12] Americans have come to this view not because they are dutifully seeking to understand God's will for their lives; instead, they have grasped dimly the fact that marriage is essentially a divinely mandated relationship. By remaining faithful to one partner, they may avoid facing God's wrath—the feature of His character that Americans acknowledge and respond to more commonly than any other.

This helps to explain why three out of four adults reject the notion that "marriage should not automatically be thought of as a permanent arrangement between two people." Most people enter a marital union with the belief that, under ideal conditions, the bonds they forge will last a lifetime. They reason that marriage will legitimize and protect a long run of mutual appreciation and caring. In essence, they assume that the odds are in their favor.[13]

SEEDS OF DOUBT

Most adults are keenly aware of the difficulties that a marriage is likely to encounter. One out of every three admits that people who get married are "fighting the odds" in their attempt to achieve a successful union. In fact, one out of five adults openly states that anyone getting married these days should expect to get divorced. (See Table 3.1 for an overview of American attitudes toward marriage.)

These fears of failure and hardship are perhaps the major reasons that 41 percent of Americans conclude it is best to cohabit before getting married. It also helps to explain why seven out of ten Americans assert that family stability can be better protected when the male and female are married legally, rather than when they simply cohabit or participate in some other temporary arrangement.[14]

At the same time, though, danger signs are everywhere. About half of all married adults say that they find their marriage to be less fun the longer they are married.[15] "When we were first married, we just

TABLE
3.1
What People Believe About Marriage

Belief	Percentage Who Agree	Percentage Who Disagree
God intended for people to get married and stay in that relationship for life.	79	18
For a family to have stability, the adults should be legally married.	70	29
If the traditional family unit falls apart, the stability of American society will collapse.	70	27
Marriage should be used by people to help them cope with life more effectively, but it should not limit a person's activities or opportunities in any way.	68	28
Our nation would be better off if getting a divorce was made more difficult.	44	53
Before getting married, it's best to live with that person for a while.	41	56
People who get married these days are fighting the odds; it's almost impossible to have a successful marriage these days.	32	66
Marriage should not automatically be thought of as a permanent arrangement between two people.	24	74
People getting married these days should expect that at some point their marriage is probably going to end in divorce.	20	77
Marriage is an outdated idea that does not fit into America's culture these days.	9	89

Source: "Family in America" survey conducted in February 1992 by the Barna Research Group, Ltd. These data reflect the answers of 1,009 people interviewed in the study. Percentages do not add to 100 percent due to respondents who gave "don't know" replies.

couldn't get enough of each other" was the explanation offered by a woman in her early thirties who is currently separated from her husband. They had married in their early twenties after an exhilarating three-year period of courtship and engagement. "But as time went on and we began to settle into a lifestyle, we increasingly got bored with each other. I still can't put my finger on what happened. All I know is that Tom was the center of my world for the first few years. Now, we seem to endure each other more than enjoy each other."

Interestingly, most people (68 percent) believe that in a successful marriage, each partner will have the freedom to do what he or she wants.[16] But the potential for conflict becomes apparent because a similar proportion of adults (68 percent) view marriage as a way of personal survival without accepting the necessity of sacrificing conflicting opportunities and activities.[17]

These views are indicative of a culture in which the demands of daily life push people to strive for personal survival, accomplishment, and pleasure rather than marital bonding and fulfillment. Research has repeatedly shown that when partners fail to have a strong mutual commitment, their marriage is likely to end in failure. Individuals who want only personal comfort, security, and pleasure frequently demonstrate less willingness to sacrifice immediate personal gratification in exchange for the longer-term stability and contentment of marriage.

"You can't really get by in a marriage unless you give up some of your own desires and dreams for the good of the desires and dreams that you both have. It really has to be a give and take deal," claimed one middle-aged woman. She had built her life around her marriage, but she had entered it with unrealistic expectations. The relationship drained her without giving her any emotional replenishment. "If you only take, you'll leave your spouse unsatisfied. It's no better if you only give, either, because you cannot give, give, give all the time without getting something in return. That was my mistake. I thought if I just keep giving, we can't go wrong. But I ran out of stuff to give. I needed to be supported, too." She reflects a trait common in our culture to fix what is broken and make it successful. "Believe me, when my first marriage broke up, not only was I devastated, but I was dead set on figuring out what went wrong and how to make my next marriage work. So far, treating this marriage as a trade-off—I give a little, I take a little, and we try to gain balance in how we interact—seems to be the trick."

The values and attitudes that people bring to a marriage strongly affect that relationship. For instance, most people would agree that romance and love are vitally important ingredients for a good marriage, but those who believe that one should marry only for financial security amount to a mere 10 percent.[18] Another common attitude today is that marriage should be put on hold until one's personal ambitions are fulfilled or at least on the way to being fulfilled. Many young adults are waiting to get married until their mid-twenties or later because they want to finish their education, pursue a career, or enjoy their freedom. Women, in particular, tend to defer marriage because they are not anxious to shoulder both career and household responsibilities too soon. With the majority of young women leaving school and directly entering the labor force, the woman who marries young and labors as a home-maker is now the aberration.

Janet is a single adult in her mid-twenties, having graduated from a small, independent college in the Northeast three years earlier. She enjoys her job in employment services and hopes to continue to climb the company ladder. "I struggled all through college, just waiting for the day I'd be in the workplace, building my career. I definitely want to get married in the next few years, but there's just no way I could have juggled a new career, independence, a marriage, and the possibility of having kids right after graduating from college." She expects to remain working, at least part-time, after she has children.

In short, people are wary of the calamities that easily and frequently challenge marriages today. But they remain optimistic about their own ability to find the right partner and sustain a positive relationship over the long haul. They also believe that having a single, long-term, healthy marriage is not merely possible, but desirable.

TIMING IS IMPORTANT

In spite of all the doubts and concerns raised about marriage, 38 percent of all adults who have never been married said they definitely want to get married, and 46 percent said they would like to under the right circumstances. Nine percent said they are not really interested in the possibility, and 5 percent said they definitely do not want to become married.[20]

Compared to the fifties and sixties, adults are waiting longer before they get married. When placed in a broader historical context, however, the statistics indicate that we are simply returning to what was normal a century ago. In 1890, the average age at which a person first married was twenty-six for men and twenty-two for women. Those averages consistently decreased until they hit twenty-three for men and twenty for women in 1960. Since that time, though, the median age has consistently crept upwards, returning to pre-1900 levels. The median age for marriages today is twenty-six for men and twenty-four for women.[21] These are close to the ages that most young adults (those eighteen to twenty-four) describe as the ideal time for people to get married: twenty-six for a man, twenty-five for a woman.[22]

Because women today are less likely to see marriage as their central life experience, their urgency to get married has diminished.

In two out of three marriages, the groom is older than the bride. In first marriages, the average age difference is about two years; in remarriages among divorced adults, the difference averages slightly over three years; marriages among widowed adults have an average age gap of nearly nine years.[23]

Timing, as in many endeavors in life, seems to be important in marriage, too. The Census Bureau has calculated, according to age, the likelihood of a person's getting married. They discovered that the longer a person waits, the less likely he or she is to tie the knot. Among women who have never been married, those who have no college education have a 65 percent chance of getting married, whereas those with a college degree have an 85 percent likelihood. By age thirty-five, if a woman is still single, she has a 32 percent chance of being wed, regardless of her educational achievements. By age forty-five, the probability of finding a mate is reduced to just 12 percent for those lacking a college degree, and 9 percent for college-educated women.

Because women today are less likely to see marriage as their central life experience, their urgency to get married has diminished. Since most Americans now accept and even condone premarital sex between consenting adults, the option of having a child without being married, the status of women in college programs and in the labor force, and the legality and desirability of cohabitation, much of the pressure to get married young no longer exists. To most adults, when it happens, it happens; there is no automatic advantage associated with getting a head start on marriage.

MOTIVATIONS FOR COMMITMENT
People get married for a vast array of reasons, some of which are routine and expected, some of which are truly odd. Commonly, however, people get married to avoid loneliness and to have someone with whom they can share emotional and physical experiences.

Among individuals who have never been married but are interested in doing so, six out of ten stated that their primary motivation for seeking a spouse was to have consistent companionship. "I really want to share my life with someone who knows me, cares about me, and will enjoy the high points of my life," one of our young female respondents explained. "It's just not as fulfilling when you do everything alone. You can tell your girlfriends about your life, but I just think it would be more meaningful to share things with your husband."

Others spoke of a longing for a permanent and reliable confidante who would be there during the good and the not-so-good times. "I'm tired of initiating everything myself, going places by myself, thinking about my experiences by myself. Sometimes I think it's great having this freedom and independence, but other times I get really sad that there isn't someone who is there to go through the good and the bad with me." After a slight pause, this successful career woman, now in her late twenties, continued, "I used to think of marriage as a crutch to get you through the hard times. But now I guess I'm seeing it more as a stabilizer. The good times don't seem as good when you can't celebrate them with somebody who can place it in your life context."

Another perspective was offered by a young man in his mid-twenties. "I grew up in a family. All of my friends had families. It's just natural. You grow up wanting what you know, and to me, family is about being together and knowing that people who understand you will be there no matter what happens. I have been out of the house for about five years now and I'm getting tired of the singleness. I'm ready to devote my time and attention to someone, and to get that quality of concern and attention back from them."

One-fourth of all never-been-married singles find love to be the most desirable part of marriage. Many discussed their yearning to express their emotions for another person in a more enduring and intimate way, apart from sexual involvement. "Sex is part of it, but I want something deeper and lasting," was the explanation of a male in his early twenties. "You can find sexual partners a lot more easily than you can find someone who really loves you. And when it comes down to what I really need, I think I could go without sex, but I can't make it without love." Other respondents spoke of finding someone with whom they could share intimate feelings.

About one out of every five never-been-married individuals feel that having children is an important part of marriage. This number, however, is lower than that of past decades. Although this finding does not necessarily mean we cherish children less in our culture, it does suggest that the desire to find personal fulfillment in marriage is a more important consideration. Many people today also believe that marriage and childbearing are unrelated activities. Note, for instance, that 40 percent of all women who give birth to their first child this year will not be married. It is increasingly accepted in America that marriage is a reasonable but purely optional precursor to having children.

Notice, too, that about one out of five respondents said that the prospect of achieving greater stability and consistency in their relationships would be a true advantage of marriage. In a nation where change is constant and success is measured by the ability to be flexible and roll with the punches, many individuals are searching desperately for some refuge of constancy. In marriage they hope to find that security.

MISSING IN ACTION

After watching today's movies and television programs, you would expect that most people marry to find sexual intimacy. The data point out, however, that surprisingly few people who have never been married list sexual involvement as a motivation for marriage. This may well be due to the fact that most people who get married these days have already been sexually active.

The figures are alarming. A majority of people have had sexual intercourse outside of marriage by the time they are nineteen. That proportion has been rising steadily, despite sex education in the public schools, the well-publicized spread of sexually-transmitted diseases, and the fatal consequences of AIDS. Nor is sexual involvement limited to a single adventure to satisfy curiosity or reduce peer pressure. Three out of ten high school seniors have had four or more sexual partners. Among people getting married for the first time this year, it is estimated that only one out of every four (28 percent) will be virgins.[24] And if the recent averages remain constant, of those who marry for the first time, almost two out of three newlyweds (62 percent) will have had sexual intercourse with someone other than their spouse prior to the marriage.[25]

Notice, too, what was not listed among people's reasons for getting married.

- Parental or family pressure to marry is minimal in modern American society. What a change from two centuries ago when a parent's duty was to arrange the marriage of his offspring.
- Cultural expectations are also far less important. In past eras, "normal" people were those who got married, and remaining single was often interpreted to mean that an individual was a failure or somehow defective. Just as marriage today does not make you a healthy person, being single no longer means you are a social reject. Today, if you

get married, it is because you choose to do so, not because it is the cultural norm. (See Table 3.2 for a more complete breakdown of the reasons people get married.)

- It is also important to note that nearly half of all marriages that take place these days involve at least one partner who is remarrying.

DOES MARRIAGE WORK?

In contrast to what the TV talk shows and tabloid press would have us believe, most married adults sing the praises of marriage. They proudly proclaim that if they had it to do all over again, they would wed the same individual. In fact, more than nine out of ten married adults (94 percent) say that most satisfying relationships they have result from their marriages—usually those with their spouses (61 percent), their children (12 percent), or their immediate family members (20 percent).

Even though the tensions and pressures felt by married people are pervasive and well-documented, most married adults are happy with their circumstances. In total, 61 percent of currently married adults say they are completely satisfied with their marriages, 31 percent claim they are mostly satisfied, and 7 percent are somewhat satisfied. Just 1 percent say they are not too or not at all satisfied with their marriages. That's more than nine out of ten adults who say that they are satisfied with their marriages.[26] Interestingly, these measures of satisfaction with marriage have not changed much in recent times, even though our culture is experiencing deep and rapid changes.

Hidden in the data are some useful insights about what causes such enthusiasm for marriage. Consider these results:

- The people who are most likely to be completely satisfied with their marriages are those in the youngest and oldest age brackets. Among married people eighteen to twenty-seven, 68 percent were completely satisfied with their union, and 66 percent of the adults forty-seven or older concurred. But just 56 percent of the married people twenty-eight to forty-six were completely satisfied. This is

TABLE
3.2

Why Singles Want to Get Married

Reason	Percent who mentioned
To have consistent companionship; someone who is there for you; someone to share your life with	60%
To be loved and receive love; to be with someone who is concerned about you	24%
To have children	21%
For stability; for security; to have deeper commitment in a relationship; having a long-term relationship	18%
To have a spouse or partner	5%
For financial security or benefit	5%
To have sexual intimacy; having a permanent partner; to have frequent sex	3%
To achieve happiness	2%

Source: "Family in America" survey conducted in February 1992 by the Barna Research Group, Ltd. These data reflect the views of the 172 adults in the study who had never been married. The percentages exceed 100 percent because each person was allowed to give multiple answers.

largely attributable to the pressures of raising children during their teenage years. In fact, whereas 70 percent of the married respondents who did not have children in their household said they were completely satisfied, only 60 percent of those with children affirmed that view. Andrew Greeley's research found a similar outcome, noting that mothers of children were less likely to express happiness with life and marriage, mainly because they could not achieve a desired balance between work, home, social needs, religious growth, and other felt needs.[27]

- Men are generally more pleased with the circumstances of their marriage than women. Overall, two-thirds of the men (66 percent) but just 56 percent of the women described themselves as completely satisfied with their marriages. Given that the greater burden for meeting the everyday needs of the family usually falls on the woman, this is not surprising, although it is significant. Perhaps unexpectedly, though, the research also shows that when married men assume greater responsibilities for household and family duties, both the husband and wife exhibit higher levels of satisfaction with their marriage. This is true both when children are present in the household and when financial pressures are evident. The sharing of responsibilities—that is, the development of a true partnership—goes a long way toward dissipating frustrations.

- The role of religious practice in a marriage is quite important. Individuals who described themselves as religious were more likely than others to cite complete satisfaction with their marriage. Those who view religion as very important in their lives were more likely to be wholly satisfied in marriage than were those who ascribed lesser value to religion. Born-again Christians, evangelical Christians, and those individuals who were more involved in personal and corporate religious behavior invariably scored higher on the marriage satisfaction scale than did those

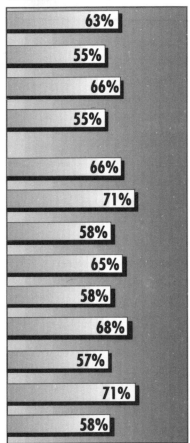

TABLE 3.3 | What Difference Does Religion Make in a Marriage?

Religious Indicator

Percentage completely satisfied with their marriage

Religious Indicator	Percentage
Describe themselves as "religious"	63%
Do not describe themselves as "religious"	55%
Say that religion is "very important" in their lives	66%
Say that religion is "somewhat," "not too," or "not at all important" in their lives	55%
Born-again Christian *	66%
Evangelical Christian **	71%
Neither evangelical nor born-again	58%
Attend church services in a typical week	65%
Do not attend church services in a typical week	58%
Read the Bible in a typical week	68%
Do not read the Bible in a typical week	57%
Discuss their religious beliefs with others	71%
Do not discuss their religious beliefs with others	58%

*In this study, "born-again Christians" were defined as people who said in our surveys they have made a personal commitment to Jesus Christ that is still important in their lives today and who said that when they die they will go to heaven because they have confessed their sins and accepted Jesus Christ as their Savior.

**In this study, "Evangelical Christians" were defined as people who responded positively to essential beliefs that evangelical Christians hold in common. The responses required for such categorization were: belief that there is one all-powerful, all-knowing, perfect God who created the universe and rules it today; agreement with the born-again Christian criteria listed in the previous paragraph; a belief that religion is very important in their lives; agreement with the statement that the Bible is totally accurate in all that it teaches; a belief that they personally have a responsibility to share their religious beliefs with others who may think differently (and have so shared their religious beliefs in the past six months); rejection of the notion that all good people, whether they consider Christ to be their Savior or not, will live in heaven after they die on earth; and a willingness to classify themselves as Protestant, Catholic, or Christian.

Source: "Family in America" survey conducted in February 1992 by the Barna Research Group, Ltd. These data reflect the answers of the 596 married adults in this study.

who committed their time and energy to other pursuits. (Table 3.3 demonstrates the correlation between religion and marital satisfaction.)

When you ask adults to define outright what makes their marriages most satisfying, the answers generally refer to the emotional bonding that takes place between husband and wife. (Table 3.4 looks at the conditions that produce satisfying marriages.) Interestingly, just 17 percent claim that their children are the greatest source of joy in the marriage. Even when the statistics are recalculated to exclude married people who do not have children, this figure rises only minimally, to 20 percent. That does not mean that children do not frequently contribute to the joys of family life. Rather, our research confirms the widely held opinion that raising children is difficult work; it bears substantial rewards and emotional satisfaction, but it can be a tough task. (See chapter 5 for a deeper discussion of the realities of parenting these days.)

In 1980, the Gallup Organization asked a national sample of adults what was most satisfying about their family life. The responses look amazingly similar to those from our 1992 study. The answers frequently mentioned relational joys and development that spouses shared; children were mentioned by only 19 percent of the respondents.[28]

THE DARK SIDE

What makes a marriage frustrating? The sources of dissatisfaction can be extensive. It seems that there is no single behavior or circumstance that produces frustration in marriage, but rather a series of problems that vary from relationship to relationship.

The most common source of marital stress is financial hardship, listed by 17 percent of married people. The emotional toll that financial pressures exert on the husband-wife relationship is often enormous and can lead to serious divisions within the marriage. In some cases, people told us the financial tension they faced was so oppressive they could not bear it much longer. In other cases, people in similar plights responded by taking on additional employment, thereby limiting the time they had for sharing important experiences. This, in turn, caused great irritation because they were unable to pursue the kind of companionship they desired from their marriage.

One survey respondent expressed the gut-wrenching pressures that his household's financial havoc created. "It has been so difficult to focus on the relational needs of my wife and kids when I can't figure out how to make ends meet financially. Sometimes I hate going home because the problems are just compounded. I already have two jobs, and we live a fairly simple life, but I'm about ready to crack under this pressure. School loans, car loans, braces for Katie, health insurance premiums, and on and on. This has really driven a wedge between my wife and me. It's just not much fun, and more and more I wonder if this is all worth the effort."

Some adults indicated that they are plagued by a conflict-riddled relationship with their spouse. About one out of every ten married people cited constant arguments, personal threats, and a general atmosphere of confrontation and mistrust as being the most frustrating circumstance in their marriage. Another 8 percent identified job or career pressures as producing the most conflict.

Perhaps most unexpected, though, was the fact that one out of every four married adults said that there was nothing in particular they found to be consistently frustrating in their marriage. Moreover, this percentage was not dominated by newlyweds, but included a broad spectrum of married adults. (See Table 3.4 for a list of the sources of frustration in marriage.)

Research has shown that what people expect often becomes a reality in their lives. One study has explored people's beliefs about what causes divorce. Married people pointed to financial problems (listed by 57 percent), getting married at too young an age (43 percent), the unwillingness for partners to accept responsibilities in the marriage (32 percent), and a decline in the religious and moral values of adults (31 percent).[29]

What makes these statistics so interesting is that it appears there is little surprise to people regarding what causes a marriage to fall apart. The experience of divorced adults and the assumptions of married and never-been-married adults are virtually identical when it comes to understanding what makes a marriage work. In other words, when people get married and experience tough times in their relationship, it should come as no surprise to them.

Satisfaction in marriage, then, corresponds directly to one's commitment to a long-term, intimate, shared experience and a willingness to sacrifice conflicting ambitions for the good of the partnership. Religion plays a key role in the shaping of a successful relationship, as does a determination to make the relationship work.

HOW CHRISTIANS CAN RESPOND

Will marriage persist in spite of alternative lifestyles, shifting attitudes, and the widespread experience of failed marriages? The answer seems to be a resounding yes.

Why? Arguments that marriage cannot withstand the heat of social change are not new. Yet marriage continues to adapt to new circumstances. The likelihood that marriage will continue is supported by the fact that most people still find marriage desirable, that the majority of people who experience a broken marriage try again, and that most married people describe their marriage as both satisfying and invaluable. Marriage works because God created it to enable men and women to relate to each other in the most intimate and enduring ways. When marriage does not work, it is not because the institution is flawed, but because the people involved have flaws.

As we close in on the next century, here are some behaviors related to marriage that I would anticipate during the coming decade, based upon what we know of people's existing behaviors, values, and attitudes.

- The marriage rate will continue to decline slowly. Ultimately, though, four out of five adults will get married at least once in their lives.
- Feeling the pressures of our fast-paced, change-driven culture, many Americans will continue to question the viability of marriage. We may see an expansion of "pluralistic ignorance," fueled by an upsurge in liberalized attitudes toward divorce and parenting.

TABLE
3.4 Satisfaction and Frustration in Marriage

Sources of Satisfaction

Percent who mentioned

The companionship or friendship with the spouse	35%
The spouse's commendable qualities	29%
The amounts of time and quality of shared experiences	18%
The children	17%
Everything about the spouse	13%
The communication between husband and wife	12%
The things they have in common	10%
Receiving such support from the spouse	7%
Family life, in general	7%
The joint spiritual journey	4%
Financial comfort and security	3%

Sources of Frustration

Percent who mentioned

Nothing; no frustrations with marriage	25%
Financial struggles, economic hardships	17%
Conflict with spouse; constant disagreements	11%
Job or career demands	9%
Bad/annoying habits or qualities of the spouse	7%
Difficulties related to raising the children	6%
Not having enough time together	5%
Expectations not being met (especially sexual)	4%
Poor communication between husband and wife	4%

Source: "Family in America" survey conducted in February 1992 by the Barna Research Group, Ltd. These data reflect the answers of 596 married adults in the study.

- Most married people who divorce will get remarried. Eventually, the average adult will experience two or three marriages during his or her lifetime (a process known as serial monogamy or sequential marriage). Such adults will strive to remain faithful to their spouses while they are married but may go through a divorce or two before identifying their "ideal" partner.
- In contrast to the pattern of the last three decades, the median age at which people get married for the first time will stop rising; it will hover in the mid-twenties for at least a few years.

In chapter 11, I provide a more extensive discussion about the qualities that contribute to a successful marriage. In the meantime, here are a few additional thoughts to consider.

One's chances of creating a strong marriage are diminished by buying into the notion that most marriages are bound to fail. It is far healthier to work on building up the positive side of marriage. By doing so, you'll recognize what most Americans have discovered: most marriages actually last and provide significant benefits to those involved. Also, be a cautious consumer of information that hails the demise of marriage and family. Be aware that much of the information offered through "news" reports, talk shows, and "investigative reporting" is based upon subjective, anecdotal evidence that often paints a far gloomier picture of marriage in America than statistics bear out.

It is also imperative that the church support those who are married. If we acknowledge that marriage was ordained by God as the appropriate means for creating families and for enabling men and women to achieve emotional and sexual intimacy, we must assume that the church bears some responsibility for keeping marriage strong. By helping spouses who are struggling and encouraging others who are making their marriages work, the church could provide an enormous gift to the stability of the nation and the satisfaction that individuals can derive from life.

As an individual called to serve God, how are you supporting marriages? The options before you are almost endless. Determine what talents and resources you can contribute, then minister in a tangible way to build marriages and families.

Notes

1. "Household and Family Characteristics: March 1991," U.S. Dept. of Commerce, Bureau of the Census, Series P-20, #458.

2. Based on a national survey of 602 adults, eighteen to twenty-nine years of age, conducted by Yankelovich Clancy Schulman in July 1990.

3. Based on a national survey of 505 adults, eighteen to twenty-four years of age, conducted by Yankelovich Clancy Schulman in October 1990.

4. These data are described in Andrew Greeley's excellent book about marriage in America, *Faithful Attraction* (New York: Tor, 1991), 21. His data are drawn from four large national surveys regarding marriage, two conducted by the Gallup Organization and two by National Opinion Research Center.

5. Frances Goldscheider and Linda Waite, *New Families, No Families* (Berkeley, Calif.: Univ. of California Press, 1991), 14.

6. Frank Magid & Associates interviewed 1,005 adults nationwide in April 1990. The results showed that 75 percent of respondents said they were very happy in their marriages, 21 percent somewhat happy, 3 percent were not happy, and 2 percent did not know.

7. Data from "Family in America" survey, conducted by Barna Research Group, Ltd., in February 1992. The national random sample size was 1,009 adults.

8. "Family in America" survey, Barna Research Group. The sample included 206 individuals who had never been married.

9. Ibid.

10. These data are taken from "Omnipoll 2-92,"conducted by Barna Research Group, Ltd. in July 1992. The national random sample size was 1,009 adults.

11. These remarks are taken from the text of a 1991 presentation delivered by Dr. Armand Nicholi, compiled in a paper entitled "What Do We Know About Successful Families." The monograph may be obtained by contacting Grad Resources, 13612 Midway Road, Suite 500, Dallas, TX 75244.

12. The actual figure found in the study was 75 percent. This study was conducted by researchers at the University of Wisconsin-Madison, Center for Demography and Ecology, as part of the National Survey of Families and Households study. The information is contained in paper #33 of this series, "Young Adults' Views of Marriage, Cohabitation and Family," by James Sweet and Larry Bumpass.

13. Nevertheless, marriage partners will also look for an escape hatch should the marriage prove to be less than ideal. The Barna Research study, "Family in America," found that 74 percent of Americans consider divorce to be the most reasonable response to crises and extenuating circumstances that injure a marriage.

14. "Family in America" survey, Barna Research Group.

15. See Greeley, *Faithful Attraction*.

16. Sweet and Bumpass, "Young Adults' Views of Marriage, Cohabitation and Family."

17. "Family in America" survey, Barna Research Group.

18. Ibid.

19. Ibid.

20. "The Statistical History of the United States and Marital Status and Living Arrangements: March 1988," U.S. Bureau of the Census.

21. This insight was derived from a Yankelovich Clancy Schulman survey conducted in October 1990 among a national sample of 505 persons in the eighteen-to twenty-four-year-old range.

22. See *Statistical Abstract of the United States, 1991* (Washington, D.C.: U.S. Dept. of Commerce, Bureau of the Census, 1991), table 131.

23. Data provided by the Centers for Disease Control and the National Center for Health Statistics, based on various studies they have conducted from 1988 through 1992.

24. Greeley, *Faithful Attraction*, 34.

25. "Family in America" survey, Barna Research Group.

26. Information drawn from the research described by Greeley in *Faithful Attraction*.

27. "American Families, 1980," American Research Corporation, Newport Beach, Calif.

28. Ibid.

29. Based upon the results of a nationwide telephone survey conducted in 1990 by Patricia Tanaka & Company. Sample size was 1,000 respondents.

CHAPTER FOUR

THE TRUTH ABOUT DIVORCE

Amerca now boasts the highest divorce rate in the world. Despite some minor fluctuations, the pattern of ruptured marriages has remained constant during the eighties and into the nineties. For Americans, the allure of divorce is that it appears to offer the simplest solution to what typically amounts to a complex web of problems. As always, appearances can be deceiving. Divorce often shatters spouses emotionally and financially. In fact, the consequences can be more harrowing than the troubled marriage.

BREAKING WITH THE PAST TO BREAK FROM THE FAMILY

Historically, most people have not had access to easy divorce. In earlier eras, when Judeo-Christian principles formed the basis of law and of personal morality, divorce was reserved for exceptional cases. Given the respect accorded to the Bible's stand on divorce (breaking up a marriage was forbidden except in cases of marital unfaithfulness), people found ways to handle their family problems apart from seeking a court-ordered separation.

Governments passed laws to protect the family. For centuries it was virtually impossible to obtain a legal divorce in most Western nations. In 1857 Great Britain finally allowed for a lawful termination of marriage under certain circumstances. Individual states in America soon added similar provisions to their own statutes, generally allowing divorce only within the confines of strict regulations and detailed procedures. Those laws gradually became less stringent, resulting in steadily growing numbers of Americans turning to divorce as their means out of an undesirable marriage.

Until 1970, divorce was not an attractive option to an estranged couple because it usually entailed expensive and emotionally painful litigation. Some discouraged adults who endured the process admitted that they experienced greater anguish, embarrassment, and emotional damage as a result of courtroom maneuvering than would ever have occurred in the marriage itself. But the rules changed dramatically in 1970 when the state of California introduced "no fault" divorce legislation. This provision required only that both the husband and wife agree before the court that their marriage was irretrievably broken. At that point, the details of the divorce arrangements could be worked out privately, and upon completion the court would certify the settlement.

The new law was hailed as a major breakthrough. Indeed it was, but not in the manner expected by many experts. Marriage counselors, ministers, psychologists, and other professionals had declared that the divorce rate would most likely plummet once the no-fault provision took effect because the issue of guilt would have no bearing on the settlement. "This law will cure quarreling adults of the 'grass is greener' perception," explained a well-known divorce attorney of the day. "Once people realize that the courts will no longer take sides and provide some type of moral victory or vindication, the motivation to seek a judicial decision will be gone. Adults will realize that they have to act like adults and work out their problems without running to the judge for a verdict." In fact, experts imagined that reconciliation between disenchanted partners would increase, since a no-fault divorce would not resolve the issue of who was right and who was wrong in the marriage.

How wrong the experts were! Not only did divorce rates in California soar, but other states that had followed the lead of the largest state experienced the same results. Record numbers of adults abandoned their 'til-death-do-us-part relationships. (Table 4.1 gives the comparative figures by year.) The notion of divorce as a liberating act was made much easier by the no-fault settlements, thus neutralizing the idea that people would avoid divorce because it had become an unsatisfying emotional stalemate.

The experts also failed to foresee the magnitude of consequences that have resulted. Recent research is unusually consistent in showing the far-reaching and invariably debilitating effects of divorce. As the Baby Boomers continue to age, there is increasing hope that the divorce rate may recede as they pass beyond the ages at which divorce is most likely to occur (early twenties to mid-thirties). The abundant evidence suggesting that divorce rarely solves the problems plaguing marriage partners is also having some impact on people's willingness to end their marriages. Even so, divorce will continue to remain a serious concern for American society and for the health and endurance of the family.

THE MYTH OF FIFTY PERCENT

Since 1980, there have been approximately 2.4 million marriages each year and roughly half as many divorces granted (about 1.2 million annually). The big jump in the frequency of divorce happened between the mid-sixties and mid-seventies. The increase was so substantial that by 1975, more marriages were ended by divorce than by the death of a spouse for the first time in the nation's history.

The rise in the incidence of divorce was quite dramatic. Whereas 393,000 divorces were granted in 1960, the total increased by 80 percent to 708,000 by 1970; it jumped again, to over one million by 1975, and has remained in the 1.1 million to 1.2 million range from 1980 to the present. These numbers mean that for every 100 marriages that took place in 1960, there were 26 divorces; in 1970, there were 33 divorces per 100 marriages; and in 1980 there were 50 divorces for each 100 marriages. In 1990, there were 48 divorces for each 100 marriages.[1]

Yet for more than a decade now Americans have been led to believe that matters are worse than they really are. Granted, the situation is serious; the divorce rate is excessive. Still, the conclusion offered by a wide array of journalists and professionals that about half of all marriages end in divorce is wrong. That calculation is twice as high as the reality. Today, only about one-fourth of Americans who have been married have also experienced at least one divorce.[2]

How did this whopping deception gain widespread credence? Largely through illogical mathematics and the unthinking acceptance of this "fact" by scholars, journalists, politicians, and public figures. The figure in question is derived by dividing the number of marriages that occur each year by the total number of divorces that happen in that same year. Since we normally have about twice as many marriages as divorces, some have concluded that approximately 50 percent of all marriages end in divorce.

But careful thinking shows this makes no sense. It's like claiming that since half of all adults are overweight and one-quarter of all adults eat pizza everyday, therefore half of all overweight adults must eat pizza everyday. The fallacy in the argument is that we're combining behavioral data for two entirely different groups of people. The people who get divorced and who get married this year are, for the most part, different people. It is not possible to claim that half of all marriages end in divorce simply because this year we had two times as many people get married as got divorced.

Think of it this way. What would happen if next year we read that one million people got married but two million got divorced? What would we conclude? That a person is twice as likely to get divorced as to get married?

Our research shows that about one-quarter of all adults who marry eventually become divorced. As divorce becomes more prevalent, the figure inches upward. However, we have a long way to go before we can proclaim that half of all marriages end in divorce. In fact, we may never reach that point.

THE DEMOGRAPHICS OF DIVORCE
Divorce, like marriage, usually occurs in early adulthood. The information shown in Table 4.1 notes that the younger a married person is, the

TABLE
4.1 **Divorce in America**

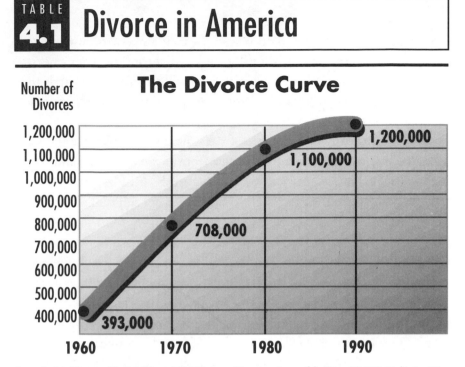

The Divorce Curve

Number of Divorces

393,000 (1960)
708,000 (1970)
1,100,000 (1980)
1,200,000 (1990)

Source: *Statistical Abstract of the United States, 1990*, U.S. Dept. of Commerce, Bureau of the Census, U.S.G.P.O., Washington, D.C., 1990.

The Divorce Rate

Age	Number of divorces per 100 married people	
	Females	**Males**
Under 20	5.09	4.98
20-24	4.66	4.99
25-29	3.51	3.82
30-34	2.77	3.08
35-39	2.37	2.60
40-44	1.91	2.26
45-49	1.28	1.71
50-54	.77	1.09

Source: *Statistical Abstract of the United States, 1990*, U.S. Dept. of Commerce, Bureau of the Census, U.S.G.P.O., Washington, D.C., 1990, p. 88. Original data reported as number of divorces per 1,000 married people.

more likely he or she is to get divorced. In fact, a majority of teenagers who get married see their relationship end in divorce. The older a person gets, the more likely it is that his marriage will survive. If a marriage is going to dissolve, it will usually happen by the time the partners reach their early forties.

Divorce is no respecter of persons, though. Neither the well-educated nor the wealthy are insulated from divorce. Studies show that such individuals are somewhat less likely than those of lesser means and schooling to suffer a divorce, but the difference is not substantial. Contrary to a common assumption, blacks are no more likely than whites to go through a divorce. Marriages collapse with roughly equal frequency in all regions of the nation, and are only slightly more common in suburban and urban settings than among rural residents. In short: divorce inflicts damage on all population groups with nearly equal frequency and ferocity.

Interestingly, the religious life of the married couple has a direct bearing on the likelihood of divorce, but the connection is not as strong as it used to be. In fact, the most recent studies indicate that people who belong to denominations that tend to campaign most vigorously against divorce—Protestants and evangelicals—actually are somewhat more likely than others to experience a marital split. The most surprising finding is that evangelicals represent 12 percent of the adult population but 16 percent of the divorced population.[3]

The prevalence of remarriage among divorced individuals is another trend of our times. Until recently, divorce usually meant that an individual would remain single for the rest of his or her life. In 1900, for instance, only 3 percent of all brides who were getting remarried had been divorced. By 1987, the latest year for which such data are available, 94 percent of all women who were getting married again had been divorced!

In fact, since the mid-eighties, a majority of all weddings have included at least one partner who has been divorced. Among all marriages that take place this year, six out of ten of those unions will involve at least one divorced person. Overall, about eight out of ten divorced men eventually remarry; slightly fewer, around seven out of ten divorced women, ultimately remarry.[4] Those remarriages occur an average of two years after the divorce becomes final.[5]

REPEATING OUR MISTAKES

Unfortunately, practice does not make perfect when it comes to marriage. Although about one quarter of all first marriages end in divorce, two out of three second or subsequent marriages eventually fail.[6] Second or subsequent marriages also last a shorter time than the first failed marriage. First marriages end after an average of seven years; subsequent unions are dissolved after an average of just five years.[7]

Some of the professionals with whom we spoke suggested that timing is critical. One expert remarked, "In my opinion, part of the problem has to do with marrying while still in the healing process. Divorce is an emotional trauma, the emotional equivalent of a bout with cancer. You can't generally expect an individual to address all of the issues involved in that trauma within the two-year period that so many people leave between the finalizing of the divorce and their next marriage."

Other analysts attribute the difficulty of second or subsequent marriages to the American determination to bury failures and master one's environment. One therapist said, "In my counseling, it seems that the people most likely to remarry within a year or two of a divorce engage in only a superficial exploration of the issues that caused the divorce in the first place. This is quite dangerous since it hikes the probability that the individual has not yet learned the crucial lessons from the first experience before moving on to the second."

Most people have difficulty suggesting anything other than a few superficial reasons why their marriage failed.

A different spin on this situation was offered by a pastor who spends nearly one-quarter of his time each week counseling people who have marriage difficulties. "Many of the adults I speak with are running from their past and would like to get into a positive, healthy relationship for a variety of good reasons. Unfortunately, until they deal with their past, the chances of developing and nurturing such a strong relationship are slim. I think part of the problem has to do with our attitude of selfishness and the unwillingness to ask God to forgive us for our personal failings and to give us the strength and wisdom to act in accordance with His will for our lives. To do so would be to truly surrender to Him, and that's a step that few people seem to take. Fewer, certainly, than the number who profess to have done so."

WHAT CAUSES MARRIAGES TO FALL APART?

The fact that marriage is a struggle for many, if not most, people is no real surprise. Professionals who study and deal with families have been describing the conflicts in marriage for literally hundreds of years. Two of the more notable were Sigmund Freud and Georg Simmel. Both argued that while tension within a marriage is unavoidable, it is healthy because the reconciliation of that tension leads to deeper intimacy and stronger relationships. Deeper emotional bonding can occur when a balance is achieved between love and antagonism.

But that balance is not easy to achieve—especially when the prevailing cultural attitudes condone and even encourage the disruption of relational commitments. In our society, we expect marriage to provide us with romance, empathy, excitement, physical gratification, and security. These expectations have become so lofty that the chances of experiencing a significant letdown are raised to dangerous levels. Faced with disappointment and pain in the wake of such a letdown, people often calculate the costs and rewards of a marriage and determine which is greater. According to this "exchange theory" of marriage, if the costs of the relationship outweigh its rewards, the marriage is doomed.

Most people have difficulty suggesting anything other than a few superficial reasons why their marriage failed. That, in itself, may help to explain why those who get remarried often find themselves in another disastrous relationship. One large-scale survey discovered that people offered broad, sweeping generalizations about the reasons for their split. Half of the divorced people interviewed stated that lack of commitment was the culprit in their marriage; one-third placed the blame on the immaturity of one or both partners (usually the other partner); one-sixth cited financial strains; and one out of every nine said infidelity was the root cause.[8]

But the underlying reasons are far more complex than such a survey suggests. Our research indicates that the most common causes of divorce are:

- unresolvable disagreement over core values
- marital infidelity
- lack of sexual satisfaction
- the demise of religious beliefs, values, and practices in people's lives
- selfishness, manifested by a couples' deliberate lack of togetherness, incompatible personal goals, and refusal to sacrifice in the best interest of the spouse—simply stated, unreasonable expectations and unwillingness to compromise
- poor quality and frequency of communication
- the acceptance of alternative lifestyles thought to deliver the same benefits as marriage, but without the costs, such as cohabitation and birth out of wedlock
- serious financial strains
- feeling smothered by the partner, resulting in lost freedom, independence, and individuality
- job demands that reduce time and enjoyment together
- the diminished socioeconomic significance of children
- the disappearance of social stigma for those who experience divorce
- increased incidents of spouse and child abuse despite widespread education about such problems
- inability to trust the spouse's fidelity
- immaturity of one or both partners, often due to getting married too early in life
- severe substance abuse

Many adults experience one or more of these symptoms at various times throughout their marriage but often choose to ignore such irritants. Over time, however, problems may fester until they erupt into an unresolvable crisis. At the time of their divorce, most couples would be able to point to several factors in this list as contributing to the downfall of their marriage.

"I think it was in 1976 or 1977 when I finally woke up to the fact that I felt dead inside. Life no longer had any thrill or meaning for me. It was the first time when I realized that I was miserable and needed a change." Martha is now in her early fifties. She had married her college boyfriend when both were still in their senior year. Trained in economics, she bore three children and went back to work when the last child entered kindergarten. "I love my children dearly, but I would never have had any kids if I could have known what a living hell I was in for. Stan was incommunicative after about our third year of marriage. I think the kids brought it on, somehow. Anyway, the more I tried to talk with him about the problem, the more he avoided me. I began to drink, I guess to ease the pain or change my environment. Of course that didn't do any of us much good. After about three years of agony, I took the kids and went to live with my mother. Stan barely responded. He said he wanted us back, but there was that hollowness in his voice, his eyes, his words."

Many professionals believe that divorce has been made easier by recent cultural changes.

Martha retained custody of the children and worked two jobs in an attempt to provide a reasonable lifestyle for the family. Now that the children are grown and gone, she still labors at two jobs, seeking to pay off the mountain of bills that accumulated over years of marginal financial times. "For the first few years after the divorce was final, we kept in touch, because I still loved Stan, but just couldn't seem to get through to him. Today I have no idea where he is or what he's up to. It was just too much to keep up that contact, too painful for me." Marriage is not in her plans. "I suppose most people get remarried, but I'm still haunted with the feelings of failure and abandonment. I don't think I could really focus on a new relationship."

Martha's experience is not unusual. Our research suggests that the most serious of the problems that lead to divorce are different core values between the partners, poor communication, financial tension, and selfishness. Although adultery has a high likelihood of causing a divorce, being caught in an adulterous relationship is not as common as these other problems.

A psychologist from Colorado explained, "A marriage is basically an attempt to make two people into one, without removing or overwhelming the unique qualities of the individuals. To accomplish this task requires two people who are deeply committed to the kind of give and take that a successful marriage demands." He went on to say, "A large number of the divorced people I counsel clearly suffered the divorce because either they or their partner, or perhaps both, were insufficiently prepared for the sacrifices they would have to make, the compromise that must take place on nonessential matters of life, and the financial hardships that they would have to work through. All of the crises in the typical marriage require that a deep commitment to sticking it out exists, and that there will be a profound level of interaction and meaningful communication taking place with regard to what they are experiencing. Unfortunately, many couples just aren't up to the challenge."

Many professionals believe that divorce has been made easier by recent cultural changes. Many adults admit that they might not have gone through with their divorce had it not been for a no-pain, instant gratification culture that esteems pleasure over responsibility and flexibility above commitment. "Look, when I considered my options, what were my choices, really?" said Sam, a warehouse supervisor from New York. "I could stay with the wife and be miserable all my life or I could go out on my own and make something of the time I've got left. What would you choose? Hey, look around. Everybody makes the same choice these days. It's not like the olden days, when you got married and stuck it out for better or worse. When it was worse, you really paid the price. But why? No reason. I'm much better off today than I would have been if I let some outdated morality determine my life." As Sam would be quick to note, the decision to leave a marriage is helped by the conveniences of modern life (fast food, laundry, yard care, child care, home security systems) that make a spouse less necessary; higher education and economic independence among women; fewer legal problems and intricacies; and the lower cost and time commitment required to obtain a divorce these days.

An informal survey of family therapists, marriage counselors, and divorce lawyers showed that an unexpectedly high proportion champion divorce as the only intelligent solution to a broken relationship. The cynical assumption would be that such advice is self-serving; counseling people to become divorced has become an industry, one that usually pays quite handsomely. It seems more likely, though, that these professionals truly believe in divorce. Many of them describe it as liberating and ultimately healing—even though this perspective is at odds with the experience of many divorced adults. Emotional trauma, financial collapse, social instability, and psychological denial are typical in the wake of a breakup. The solution to one problem, unfortunately, often creates a host of new, sometimes devastating problems.

IT'S A PROCESS

Upon experiencing a divorce, a person usually experiences emotional upheaval. Counselors tell us that divorce commonly triggers such feelings as anger, loss, grief, jealousy, betrayal, relief, guilt, humiliation, depression, rejection, confusion, rage, and abandonment. The duration of this phase varies greatly from person to person and often depends upon the professional or personal support that the individual receives from others.

Judith Wallerstein, a well-known divorce counselor, contends that divorced adults go through three distinct stages after a divorce. The initial stage is characterized by acute unhappiness and confusion. Adults often experience a level of sexual impulsiveness that is foreign to their past. They may even erupt in fits of physical violence against their ex-partners. It is a time of great instability in their lives. The second stage begins when the adult starts to experiment with new lifestyles and forms of family support. The individual may change residence a number of times as he or she attempts to test new ways of living and search for satisfying adventure. These novel experiences enable the person to distance himself or herself from the hurt of the past and establish a new identity and purpose in life. In the final stage, the individual achieves a renewed sense of stability, contentment, and security. This is often spurred by the initiation of new, significant relationships.[9]

The life of Bill Jaymes, an accountant in his early forties, is reflective of Wallerstein's findings. He had been married just two years when he began to doubt his choice of mate. When he raised his concerns about the relationship, his wife agreed to join him in marriage counseling. Even so, they wound up divorcing after about a year of counseling sessions. Although the divorce was relatively friendly, he moved out of state and tried to begin a new life.

His experience was rocky from the start, though. He lost his first job because his attendance was sporadic. Even when he was at work, he was often unable to concentrate on the tasks at hand. "I sat there, staring at my office wall, recalling some of the exchanges Sharon and I had. I was unbelievably depressed. I had little sense of being at a job. Work was the farthest thing from my mind at that point."

He tried to overcome his grief by dating virtually any woman he met. "Talk about out of control. Anything with a skirt was fair game to me. Half the time I didn't care if the woman was married or not. The potential for compatibility was not in my decision-making criteria. I just felt compelled to erase Sharon and my relationship from my mind, and I guess I figured that increasing my pool of experiences would water down the importance of our marriage. Sure, I felt that eventually, when I met the right person, that would rewrite my history."

After being fired, Bill got involved with a divorce recovery group that met at a church in a nearby community. "Now that was a major step for me, even admitting that I was not up to dealing with things on my own. The group enabled me to move through the pain and feelings of guilt to a new level of self-confidence." He moved to yet another state and tried to begin anew. Three years brought several failed attempts at relationships, another lost job, and an arrest for drunken driving. It was at that point that Bill befriended a small group of divorced men he discovered through a contact at a professional meeting. Buoyed by the camaraderie and emotional support of those individuals, Bill's life stabilized somewhat. While he admits to being lonely, he believes that he is on the "road to recovery. These last five years have been horrendous. But maybe the grief and the pain were necessary for me to adopt a fresh perspective on myself, on relationships, and on the nature of my goals for life."

The research conducted by Wallerstein and her colleagues indicates that there is no guarantee that an individual will necessarily move beyond depression and disorientation and into the second or third stage after a divorce. Some people get stuck in the initial stage, others in the second stage. Even those who move through all three stages and exhibit personal growth do so at different, highly personal rates.

NO ONE GOES UNCHANGED
Those who go through a divorce typically indicate that the process has left its mark on all areas of their lives. From their own self-concept to views on marriage and family, from goals and values in life to religious beliefs and practices—all are affected by the breakup of a marriage.

Divorce, however, may produce fewer fundamental changes than we might expect. It appears that a divorced individual does not view the world, people, marriage, and family much differently than a person who is currently married. Although the research does not enable us to infer whether the differences that are evident were caused by the divorce or predated that event, the remarkable similarity of the divorced to the never-been-divorced segment is itself a significant revelation.

Consider, for instance, how adults view themselves. (Table 4.2 provides more detail on this matter.) The only differences among the dozen attributes we tested are that divorced adults are more likely to say they are lonely (22 percent admitted to this), marginally less likely to describe themselves as Christian (although four out of five do so), and a bit more likely to say they are skeptical. The major difference in self-perception is that many fewer divorced adults say that they lead a "traditional lifestyle"; this characterizes the behavior of nine out of ten married people, but just six out of ten divorced adults.

TABLE
4.2 **How Married and Divorced People View Themselves**

Description of Self	Married	Divorced
Lonely	6%	22%
Stressed-out	28%	25%
Born-again Christian	38%	40%
Aggressive personality	43%	40%
Too busy	50%	44%
Skeptical	65%	71%
Easy to please	65%	67%
Conservative politically	67%	70%
Religious	68%	69%
Outgoing	77%	75%
A Christian	86%	80%
Leading a traditional lifestyle	88%	63%

Source: "Family Views and Support" study conducted in March 1992 by the Barna Research Group, Ltd. These data reflect the answers of 132 divorced adults and 699 married adults.

"Why would my values or self-view be any different?" asked Wanda Rothstein, a mother of two whose divorce was finalized several years ago. "I'm the same person, but I've been through some tough times. I made a bad choice when it came to who I chose to marry. That doesn't mean I'd think differently about myself. I'm more cautious now in who I date and how I spend my emotional energy, but I still have the same convictions and see the world the same as before." When told that many marriage counselors believe a person's self-view undergoes a significant change after a divorce, she rejects the notion. "I've been through it, I should know. A mistake is one thing. But to blame myself forever and ever, or to turn my view of the world upside down because of that mistake, doesn't make sense. I'm comfortable with who I am and how I fit in the world."

We can detect a similar theme when studying a divorced person's perception of life. When we asked married and divorced adults to react to each of eighteen statements about the nature of life these days, we discovered few major differences. Divorced adults are more likely to say that their first responsibility in life is to themselves, more likely to agree that everything in life is negotiable, and less likely to say that life, in general, is very satisfying for them.[10] When asked to comment on their confidence in each of nine major social institutions, both groups had very similar responses. Divorced people are, however, less likely to be registered to vote (68 percent are, compared to 84 percent among married adults). Their political views are slightly more liberal on issues, but their stands on finances and economy, domestic and social policy, and foreign and international affairs are quite similar to those of married people.

Interestingly, we found no trace of the anger and resentment toward society that one might expect from people who had been through a marital breakup. The percentage of divorced people who expressed a lack of confidence in institutions was no higher than the percentage of married individuals who did. When they indicated a concern about the moral or ethical character of the nation, it paralleled the views expressed by married adults. The only noticeable difference was that divorced people demonstrated a slightly higher degree of belief that you must protect yourself and not take everything and everyone at face value. But even that divergence from married people was minor.

Religion plays a surprisingly minor role in the entire divorce process.

When describing what they expect or want in the future, divorced adults again show only slight differences from married people. Those who have experienced the dissolution of their marriage are more interested in obtaining a high-paying job. (Most adults endure a substantial cut in income after a divorce; women, on average, experience about a 70 percent reduction immediately after a court settlement.) They are somewhat less interested in being part of a local church and slightly more attracted to not having to work for a living. However, the value placed upon friendships, religious beliefs, integrity, interpersonal influence, health, and comfort are virtually indistinguishable from the responses offered by married adults. Even descriptions of what is important in their lives are nearly identical between divorced and married people. Divorced adults place a higher value on their time and on living comfortably, and a slightly higher value on community, career, money, and politics.[11]

Throughout our analysis it became apparent that after a person has been divorced and then remarries, those attitudes that might have changed as a result of the divorce return to their prior state. Thus, both marriage and divorce do appear to have some impact on people's views of the world, although the impact is not as considerable as we might have expected.

THE ROLE OF RELIGION

Religion plays a surprisingly minor role in the entire divorce process. One might expect that a person's religious faith would be a comfort and a strength during the marital breakup. That is apparently not the case. On the one hand, most divorced adults retain the religious beliefs they possessed prior to their divorce. On the other hand, they are less likely to practice their spirituality after the split. Divorced respondents have indicated that they cling to their beliefs as a source of strength but were surprised to find that their fellow believers were quick to judge and slow to support them during the course of their marital problems.

"I'm not one of those who goes around crying that the church is full of hypocrites and two-faced liars," declared Betty. She grew up in a churchgoing family and remained an active member in her Presbyterian church during her marriage. "What hurt me, though, and it hurt deeply, was how quickly the people who I thought were my friends felt they had to distance themselves from me once we announced that we were getting divorced. What turned me off was that there was such a pompous, holier-than-thou attitude about my suffering."

Betty talks for a few minutes about what it's like going through a divorce—the self-doubt, the loneliness, the sense of loss. Then she turns her attention back to the disappointment she felt when her church reacted negatively to her divorce. "I turned to the church, and my friends in it, for support—not asking them to condone the separation, but to at least help me through the toughest time of my life. What I got was a lot of mini-sermons about the sanctity of marriage and the sin of divorce. Do they really think I was unaware of that? Were they just trying to score points with God as His defenders? Anyway, their rejection of me has led me to leave active church life. I love God and know He loves me, in spite of the divorce. I'm just ashamed that the church couldn't reflect His love in the same way."

In assessing religious beliefs, we found that married and divorced adults exhibited only minor differences in their religious views. The frequency with which they practiced their religion, though, was another story: the gap was of Grand Canyon proportions.

- Sixty-one percent of married adults say they attend religious services three times or more each month, but only 43 percent of the divorced make the same claim.
- Sixty-two percent of the married adults say they read the Bible in a typical week. Just 48 percent of the divorced keep up the same habit.

- Among the married, 12 percent who currently attend a church say they are likely to change from that church to a different one. Among the divorced, 35 percent say they anticipate making a change.
- Married adults are twice as likely as the divorced to teach a Sunday school class at their church and three times as likely to serve in a leadership capacity at their church.

Of particular interest, though, is the fact that divorced adults do not turn their back on religion, but they often reject the local churches to which they belonged. We also found that divorced adults are every bit as likely as married people to watch religious television programs, listen to Christian radio programs, read Christian books, discuss their religious beliefs with other people, and pray to God—yet they do so outside of the realm of the organized church.

RELATIONSHIPS AND FAMILY: NEW VIEWS?

It would not be surprising to learn that divorced adults radically alter their views about relationships, marriage, parenting, and family in the wake of a difficult marriage and breakup. Yet, the way divorced adults regard relationships varies amazingly little from the way married people do. Their confidence in people, perceptions of the basic goodness of human beings, commitment to "quality time" rather than "quantity time" in building relationships, desire to have close friends, and their fears about the impact of a rapidly changing culture on relationships are almost indistinguishable from the views of the married population. Divorced adults are, however, somewhat more inclined than are married adults to say that it is very unlikely for a man and a woman to have a deep, lasting friendship without it becoming a sexual relationship. This pessimism may be a consequence of experiencing a marriage that has been shattered by the adulterous behavior of one of the partners.

But the pain and suffering is more evident when discussing marriage and family. Divorced adults clearly take a more defensive, be-prepared-for-the-worst perspective on marriage. Although they are more supportive of cohabitation as insurance against marital failure, and are more than twice as likely to say that divorce is the inevitable outcome of any marriage, they have not given up on the importance of marriage and family stability. They remain persuaded that marriage is meant to be permanent. (See Table 4.3 for additional details.)

Two out of three divorced adults maintain that American society will suffer significant damage if the traditional family unit is destroyed. And most of these individuals reveal an interest in getting married again. One-quarter of the divorced adults we interviewed said that if they had a second chance, they would marry the same person again (23 percent); 38 percent said they would marry someone else instead; 15 percent said they would forgo marriage but live with someone they loved; and 20 percent said they would remain single and live alone.

THE CHILDREN SUFFER

Most divorced adults (61 percent) indicate that the split of their families has had a negative effect on their children, whereas 31 percent say it has not had any demonstrable impact, and 7 percent say the divorce had a favorable effect on their children. "Probably the worst part of this whole ordeal has been what it has done to my kids," said a woman who walked away from her husband two years earlier. "I don't know what the long-term effects will be, but they aren't going to be positive. The decision to divorce weighed heavily on me beforehand. Now, seeing the difference it has made in the kids' behavior, I'm not sure it was the right move." Many parents indicate that the most difficult post-divorce reality has been helping their children cope with the shock that Mommy or Daddy wasn't going to be around anymore.

While divorced adults are likely to suggest that it is more difficult to raise children today than in the past and that parenting takes a lot of time and money, 84 percent argue that having children has brought them greater enjoyment in life. "Even though this has been a very hard experience for my kids, they have been the one thing that I have to hang on to which says the marriage wasn't a total mistake," remarked Mary, whose marriage lasted a decade, then ended in bitterness. "Maybe Jack and I didn't do well together, but we sure produced two beautiful and wonderful children. More than anything, they make

TABLE
4.3
The Divorced Are More Cautious About Marriage

Statement About Marriage	Married	Divorced
God intended for people to get married and to stay in that relationship for life.	80%	76%
If the traditional family unit falls apart, the stability of American society will collapse.	76%	67%
For a family to have stability, the adults should be legally married.	75%	62%
Marriage should be used by people to help them cope with life more effectively, but it should not limit people's activities or opportunities in any way.	66%	72%
Before getting married, it's best to live with that person for a while.	34%	46%
People who get married these days are fighting the odds; it's almost impossible to have a successful marriage these days.	30%	42%
Marriage should not automatically be thought of as a permanent arrangement between the two people.	22%	22%
Anyone getting married these days should expect to get divorced at some point.	15%	36%

Source: "Family in America" survey conducted in February 1992 and Omnipoll 2-91 conducted in July 1991 by the Barna Research Group, Ltd.

my life worth continuing." For most adults who see their marriage dissolve, the children produced by the union are a reminder of the benefits that even a bad marriage can produce.

Divorced adults are usually optimistic about their capability for being good parents and raising successful, well-adjusted children. They remain more accepting of unmarried parents who cohabit and have children and less convinced of the value of an unhappily married couple staying together simply for the sake of the kids.

When it comes to being tangibly involved in the lives of their children, though, the experience of divorced people differs markedly from that of married adults. As outlined in Table 4.4, divorced adults are less likely to spend time with their youngsters in seven of the eight activities surveyed than are married parents. It is important to note, though, that both married and divorced parents are equally likely to spend at least thirty minutes at a time talking with their children during the course of a week.

Research makes clear that children suffer greatly when parents decide to split up. Children of divorce generally receive less care and discipline from the remaining parent, are less adept at play with schoolmates, suffer from worse health, have a greater tendency to exhibit emotional and sexual problems as well as antisocial behavior, have a more negative outlook on the world, and lack any identification with role models. They are likely to be chronically unhappy; to feel a deep sense of loneliness and rejection; and to crave structure in their lives.[12] "Young children, especially, go through a tremendous amount of turbulence when the parents divorce," was the perspective of a prominent midwestern counselor. "Even in the homes where the parent who retains custody devotes substantial time, attention, and love to the children, there will be permanent scars on those children. You cannot rip away strong emotional attachments without leaving tear marks. Sometimes they heal better than others, but there is always a lingering scar."

Although many adults seek divorce because they believe it offers them a second chance for a good life, children of divorce are more likely to view the experience as a time of loss. They often persist in the hope that their parents will yet reconcile; they would rather live through

TABLE **4.4**

How Parents Spend Time with Their Children

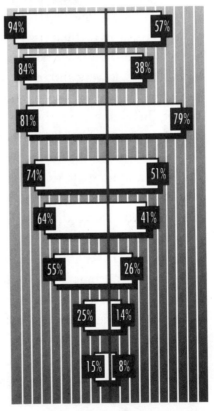

Activity

	Married	Divorced
Watch television together	94%	57%
Do homework or other educational activities	84%	38%
Spend more than 30 minutes at a time talking about life together	81%	79%
Go out for a fun meal together	74%	51%
Drive or travel to a special place that would be of interest to the kids	64%	41%
Play a sport together	55%	26%
Experience a cultural activity together, such as a museum, zoo, or play	25%	14%
Go to a movie theater together	15%	8%

Source: "Family in America" survey conducted in February 1992 by the Barna Research Group, Ltd.

a bad marriage than to go through the separation anxieties and related tribulations of a divorce.

Research among youths indicates that one of their greatest fears is that their parents will divorce. One national study of children eight to seventeen years of age found that four out of ten articulated this as a major concern.[13] Nearly 42 percent of all people eighteen to twenty-nine years of age whose parents were divorced said that the experience affected them a great deal, and another one-fourth said it impacted them some.[14] Four out of five young adults also express the fear that people in their own generation will be more likely than those of their parents' generation to get divorced.[15]

One of the major reasons Baby Busters are the most pessimistic generation in our nation's history is that they have felt the sting of divorce more than any prior generation. More than half of them lived in a family that went through a divorce, and more than four out of five had close friends whose parents split up.[16] These experiences have colored their fears about their own future. "I am gun-shy about marriage now. You see so many people who you thought were strong, loving, capable people who wind up calling it quits. What's to make me think I'll be any different? It scares me to think that some day I may have to go through the same hurt that my parents went through. It certainly has made me think twice about options to marriage."

HOW CHRISTIANS CAN RESPOND

Will divorce continue at the same pace in the years ahead? For those who have witnessed the painful consequences of divorce, it is even more sobering to see the research that shows a majority of adults, both married and divorced, reject the notion of making divorce more difficult to obtain. In fact, more than half of all married adults and about two-thirds of those presently divorced expect legal changes in the near future that will make it easier for people to do whatever they wish regarding family and parenting practices.[17]

The divorce rate in the near future will be shaped by contrasting trends in demographics and values. The aging of our population may gradually slow the divorce rate. At the same time, however, the perpetuation of values that support a "me first" lifestyle will encourage people to cash in relationships when they demand too much compromise, sacrifice, or pain. The effects of these trends may well cancel each other out, leaving our divorce rate relatively constant for the coming decade.

We can expect that the majority of divorced adults will continue to remarry, and that a majority of those remarried individuals will again find themselves ending the relationship. And it is reasonable to anticipate a generation of cynical, fearful young adults who enter marriage with deeper fears and more reservations than ever before. Most of them will opt for marriage at some point, but their fear that the relationship will fail will become a self-fulfilling prophecy for many, contributing to our society's string of broken marriages.

If divorce is here to stay, we must consider the appropriate Christian response.

First, churches and individuals who love Christ must extend their hearts to people who go through a divorce. Divorce ought not be the first recourse to marital difficulties, naturally, but we are called to love all people as God does, regardless of their lifestyles and perspectives. A divorced person is often an individual with significant needs that sympathetic and concerned people can address. Christ's love and healing can be demonstrated powerfully to those who experience marriage crises and breakups.

Second, we must invoke the power of prayer as we strive to heal our nation's families. Divorce is a cruel weapon that divides the church and families and saps the very strength from our nation. Will you pray consistently for the marriages of friends, family, and the leaders in your church, schools, community, and nation?

Third, increase your awareness. If you are married, or plan to become married, study what causes relationships to fall apart. Nobody enters a marriage with the intention of allowing it to disintegrate, yet it often happens through neglect or selfishness. You stand a better chance of preventing a divorce in your own life by learning from the mistakes and experiences of others. Develop intelligent strategies to minimize discord and build a fulfilling marriage.

Perhaps you have already been through the shock and disruption of a divorce. If you are currently trying to work through that change in your life, you may find comfort and strength through discussing your pain and bonding with other adults of the same sex who are working through the same trials. By sharing frustrations and victories, a group can form a supportive community that helps each individual emerge from the depression and self-doubt that often follows a divorce.

Notes

1. Marriage and divorce statistics are accumulated and reported by the National Center for Health Statistics in Washington, D.C. These numbers come from their data as reported in *Statistical Abstract of the United States, 1991* and from their data released in 1990.

2. "Singleness in America," Statistical Brief, U.S. Dept. of Commerce, Bureau of the Census, SB-4-89, November 1989.

3. Data from the "Family in America" and "Family Views and Support" studies, conducted in 1992 by the Barna Research Group, Ltd. See Preface for the definition of "evangelical" used in these surveys.

4. *Statistical Abstract of the United States, 1991* (Washington, D.C.: U.S. Dept. of Commerce, Bureau of the Census, 1991), table 131, p. 87.

5. Arlene Skolnick and Jerome Skolnick, *Families in Transition*, 6th ed. (Glenview, Ill.: Scott, Foresman, 1989), 112.

6. Information provided by Singles Ministry Resources, P.O. Box 62056, Colorado Springs, CO 80962-2056, in a May 1991 release; based upon data supplied by the National Center for Health Statistics.

7. Skolnick and Skolnick, *Families in Transition*, 112.

8. Research Alert, *Future Vision* (Naperville, Ill.: Sourcebooks Trade, 1991), 43.

9. Results taken from "Omnipoll 1-91," "Omnipoll 2-91," and "Omnipoll 2-92," conducted by Barna Research Group, Ltd.

10. "Omnipoll 1-92," Barna Research Group.

11. Judith Wallerstein and Sandra Blakeslee, *Second Chances* (New York: Ticknor & Fields, 1989). See especially chapter 1.

12. Such insights are gleaned from a wide variety of sources. Among the most accessible are Wallerstein and Blakeslee's *Second Chances* and Skolnick and Skolnick's *Families in Transition*. A growing list of professional journal articles and studies support such findings.

13. See the "American Chicle Youth Poll," conducted by the Roper Organization for the American Chicle Corporation and published by Warner-Lambert Co., Morris Plains, N.J., 1987. Sample of 1,000 people, eight to seventeen years of age.

14. These figures come from a telephone survey among 160 young adults, ages eighteen to twenty-nine, whose parents were divorced. The survey was taken by Yankelovich Clancy Schulman in July 1990.

15. These figures come from a national telephone survey of 505 adults, eighteen to twenty-four years old, conducted by Yankelovich Clancy Schulman in October 1990.

16. See George Barna, *The Invisible Generation: Baby Busters* (Glendale, Calif.: Barna Research Group, 1992). For a copy of this book, write Barna Research Group, P.O. Box 4152, Glendale, CA, 91222-0152.

17. "Family in America" survey, Barna Research Group.

CHAPTER FIVE

PARENTING ISN'T CHILD'S PLAY ANYMORE

Americans take great pride in their children and staunchly maintain that parenting is one of the most fulfilling responsibilities an adult can assume. Yet, what parents say and what they actually do can be riddled with inconsistencies. Consider the following contrasts:

- A common reason for marrying, and one of the major sources of satisfaction among couples, is having and raising children. Yet, fewer couples are choosing to have children these days; those who do are having fewer children.
- It is widely thought that having children brings the parents closer together. However, the divorce rates among childless couples and those who have children are not much different.
- Most adults say their goal is to share their childraising responsibilities equally with their spouses. Comparatively few actually do so.

- Our society believes that special education is necessary to enhance our performance in the most important tasks in life. But there are no special courses or training required—and surprisingly little is even available—to assist parents in their child-raising tasks.

- One of the common reasons for divorce filed with the courts is that the separation is for "the good of the children." The evidence is overwhelmingly clear, though, that children generally suffer ill effects from divorce.

- Although parents are spending more money on child-related services, toys, and education, the incidence of child abuse and the amount of time in which kids are deposited in child care are also rising precipitously.

We are seeing new trends affect parenting today. Some of these changes are a welcome breakaway from the mistaken notions of the past; some raise serious questions about the effects this style of parenting will have on the generation we are preparing for the future.

FEWER KIDS ARE ON THE WAY

Adults are having fewer children than they used to. In 1800, the average family had seven children. That figure had been sliced in half by 1900, to 3.56 children per family. By 1950, it had dropped to just 1.9; by 1990, the figure had reached a low of 1.4. This means that American adults are not even producing enough new citizens to replace themselves. Unless the trend is reversed soon (and unless immigration levels are allowed to climb upward), we can expect to see America's population decline in the early decades of the twenty-first century.[1]

It is not likely that this trend will be reversed soon. The two best measures for determining such predictions—parents' personal expectations regarding their family size and their optimism about the future—suggest that we may experience occasional upswings in the birth rate, but the average is not likely to rise above 2.1 children per family (the population replacement level) for quite some time. Census Bureau studies show that women ages eighteen to thirty-four had planned to have an average of 1.69 children apiece in 1975; 1.61 in 1980; and just 1.46 in 1988. Historically, these estimates have been quite close to the actual child-bearing record of women, intimating that women do not plan to have larger families in the near future.

The attitudes of the Baby Busters, who are now rapidly approaching the prime of their fertility, indicate that we have no reason to anticipate larger family units than we have today. The Busters are worried about their future financial status, the safety of the world's children, overpopulation and its effect on the environment, and they question their own ability to raise healthy, functional children success-fully.[2] "How did they do it?" asked one woman in her early twenties, reacting to the large families of the past. "I don't have any kids yet, and the thought of having any is just overwhelming. The world is so out of control these days, it seems insane to think about having a whole tribe of kids. One kid, maybe, but three or four, like most of our parents had, just seems out of the question. I want to enjoy my life—or at least to have a manageable life. Kids may be great, but they do rob you of your freedom and energy. I don't know if it's fair to them, given the world's conditions, and I don't feel that it'd be fair to me to have a big family."

LESS COULD MEAN MORE

Just because our society is producing fewer children is not necessarily a measure of failure or defeat. Some analysts propose that smaller families could result in a better quality of life for kids since youngsters could reasonably expect to benefit from more of their parents' time, energy, money, and experiences. "In a selfish society," explained one sociologist, "the fewer people in the picture, the greater the possibility for more meaningful relationships. Since time is a precious commodity, the fewer people that commodity has to be shared with, the better off those people are likely to be."

But a burning desire to enhance the lives of children is hardly the bottom-line motivation behind the trend toward fewer children. Heading the list of reasons parents are having fewer youngsters are the following:

■ marriages are happening later in people's lives, reducing the number of prime child-bearing years for parents

- the increase in the number of women who are working and have chosen, at least temporarily, to place their careers above parenting
- socioeconomic changes that have made child labor less necessary to the survival of the family
- the demise of the notion that large families are prestigious, replaced by the "politically correct" view that large families are irresponsible
- the increase of couples who are infertile, now estimated to be about one in five
- the popularity of abortion as a way of avoiding parenthood, resulting in the deaths of 1.4 million unborn children per year
- more effective contraception methods
- the cost of raising a family (currently estimated to cost between $100,000 and $200,000 per child for all of the child's expenses through age eighteen)

HARD WORK

Recent surveys concur that more than four out of five adults believe it is more difficult to raise children today than when their parents were raising them. Parenting has become so burdensome to many adults that they feel virtually paralyzed by the weight of the decisions they must make. They are confronted by laws that have increasingly restricted the autonomy of parents, scientific research that has shown how improper parenting can create long-term dysfunctional behavior in children, and disputes over education and how to instill proper values in youngsters. It is not surprising that a 1990 survey by NORC discovered that 85 percent of the respondents believe that "parents often feel uncertain about what is the right thing to do in raising their children." And if there is one condition that makes Americans uncomfortable, it is uncertainty. It often triggers avoidance behavior, which in this case means not having children (or having fewer of them).[3]

When Sally Dumas married her husband, she was a recent college graduate, anxious to have a family. One of six children, she was raised in the Midwest. Although she believed six kids would be too many, she thought four might be ideal. Time has changed her perspective. "The more Wayne and I studied the pressures of raising kids today, the more we were convinced that we should wait longer before having kids, and maybe have only one or two." They now have a five-year-old boy but admit that they are cautious about having another child; meanwhile, the biological clock is pressing the issue. "We love Brian. Having him was a great decision. But this is no easy job. He has worn us out more than we expected. I'm not sure that we're up to having another child."

They are not alone in their feeling that parenting is tough—probably tougher than it has ever been. "A century ago, life was hard but parenting was much easier. People didn't have all the tensions and the choices that we have to deal with today," said Ellen, a mother of three boys. Her husband left her, and she has been living for some time with a man two years her junior. She thinks back over her ten years as a parent and recalls the struggles she has endured, both as a married parent and as a single parent. "Everyday, you face tough choices, not just for yourself, but for these little ones. And it never ends. One decision after another, one crisis after another. There are many joys in parenting, of course, but there just isn't much help or support in this process. You go to work, there's supervisors or executives who can offer advice. You play sports, you have coaches. Parenting? You're on your own. I wish there was some type of precedent you could follow as you went along, but the truth is you're always on your own, doing seat-of-the-pants parenting."

When asked to see the future through a child's eyes, many parents express fear or concern. Most adults believe that the best years to have been a child were those between 1950 and 1990; just 8 percent say the days yet to come will be the best for children. Of course, nostalgia and the comfort of the known partly explains why people chose a time in the recent past as the best time for children. But an even more important consideration is that people expect the future to be characterized by deteriorating moral conditions, new family stresses, and other personal tensions. This new age of anxiety clearly deters people's interest in having children.[4]

WHAT GOALS DO PARENTS HAVE?

As parents struggle to instill a sense of accomplishment in raising their children, it is informative to learn exactly what they are seeking to create in their children.

A study by the Roper Organization determined that the trait mentioned most often by adults as being important for children to possess is having a sense of responsibility. This was the only attribute identified by at least half of all adults (it was mentioned by 63 percent). Other characteristics deemed laudable were having good manners (mentioned by 49 percent); being tolerant (45 percent); possessing a meaningful religious faith (36 percent); being independent (29 percent); being thrifty (13 percent); being loyal (12 percent); and having a healthy imagination (10 percent).[5] Interestingly, most parents think that they are doing an above-average job of raising their kids, but they usually do not measure their effectiveness by the way their children match up with the traits listed above.[6] In some ways, then, what parents describe as being important for a child may not correspond to the qualities their own kids possess. But they generally accept their children as they are, a testimony to the enduring quality of parental love.

WHO'S REALLY RAISING OUR CHILDREN?

How do you raise kids these days? The extended family generally is not available to lend a helping hand. In most households, both parents work. And who has the time to read Dr. Benjamin Spock's classic 800-page manual on childrearing?

While the public debate rages over who has the greatest influence on the development of our children, parents themselves offer some useful insights. For starters, we learned that three-quarters of all adults assert that "these days, most kids are influenced more by the schools, government, media, and other sources than they are by their parents." This is a sentiment echoed by many young people themselves.

Of course, most adults say that parents *should* have the most influence on their children. What may be most surprising, though, is whom parents identify as the single biggest influence on their kids: other kids. Other significant influences are parents and the mass media.

Schools rate fourth. Churches and the government are rarely mentioned as having much influence.[7] (See Table 5.1 for a list of the most important influences.)

Statistics like this certainly raise a long list of questions. Why aren't churches playing a bigger role in the process? What can be done to enhance the impact of parental influence? How can the influence of the media be moderated? What kind of values are being taught by those groups outside of the family? Although these complex questions are difficult to answer accurately, we must address them, for the implications are profound.

Those who warn that parents don't spend enough time inculcating values and sharing time with their families are often written off as ignorant fundamentalists, out-of-touch conservatives, or pontificating moralists. But their perspective, alarming and uncomfortable as it may be for some, cannot be easily dismissed, given the weight of the evidence that confirms their contention. For instance, a number of scholarly studies have noted kids draw most of their information from the television, spending an average of more than 10,000 hours watching it by the time they reach age eighteen. (That, by the way, represents more than one entire year—twenty-four-hour days, seven days a week—absorbing the messages broadcast by television producers.)[8] The typical child in the preschool through sixth-grade age group watches in excess of thirty hours of television programming per week.

Many adults seem baffled and even frustrated when trying to weigh the benefits and drawbacks of child care.

Further diminishing the input of parents is the extended time kids spend in school. The typical child in 1880 attended school 80 days per year; today, most states have a school year that lasts about 180 days. Preschool experience used to be uncommon; today, six out of ten children attend preschool classes prior to enrolling in kindergarten.[9]

THE SURROGATE CAREGIVERS

Financial pressures, job opportunities for women, and the pressures of time have caused millions of families to turn to professionals for help with raising their children. Child care services have become big business in our country. Currently, Americans spend more than $16 billion each year for child care.[10] Yet the quality of the attention given children and the effect of this surrogate care on their development varies significantly. Many adults are beginning to question the wisdom of such arrangements. One-third of the adults we interviewed (32 percent) said they believe that even when a child is enrolled in a good child-care facility, the experience "can leave long-term, negative effects on the child."[11]

Many adults seem baffled and even frustrated when trying to weigh the benefits and drawbacks of child care. "Look, I can either take care of them myself, twenty-four hours a day, or I can get help from a good child-care center. If I do it all myself, we won't have a lot of the extras, because we'll be financially strapped," declared Phyllis, who currently works as a hairdresser at a local salon. She, her husband, and two young children live in a modest home in a suburban Illinois community. "If I continue to work and put the kids in the day care center, they're exposed to other authority figures whose values may be significantly different from mine. The kids might grow up resenting the fact that I 'abandoned' them during the days. It feels like a no-win situation to me. Sometimes I get really depressed over it, other times I get angry that my husband doesn't make enough money for me to stay home with the kids." Phyllis and her husband have a combined income of $35,000. Without her contribution, it would be pared down to about $22,000. "The most frustrating part of it all, though, is that after I pay the day care bill, my earnings are practically back to zero," she laments.

Indeed, one of the issues that stymies so many parents is how to choose between two unsatisfying alternatives. In one of our surveys we asked adults to imagine a family in which a married couple had two children under the age of 12 living in the home. We asked respondents to indicate if they believed the children were more likely to be happy and content if the children were placed in a child-care center while both parents worked or if one parent should stay home with the children

TABLE 5.1	Who Has the Most Influence on Our Children?

Source of influence	Who or which **should** have the most influence	Who or which **does** have the most influence
Parents	97%	30%
Churches	21%	1%
Schools	1%	13%
Friends and peers of the child	*	33%
The media	*	21%
Government policies	0%	1%

Source: "Family in America" survey conducted in February 1992 by the Barna Research Group, Ltd. These data reflect the answers of 1,009 people interviewed in the study. The asterisk * denotes less than one-half of one percent.

Which Parent Spent the Most Time with the Children When They Were Young?

Area of responsibility	Parent who spent the most time		
	Mother	**Father**	**Both equally**
Caring for the health needs	71%	7%	22%
Discussing religion	48%	11%	35%
Talking about life	48%	12%	38%
Disciplining	43%	22%	34%
Playing games	42%	17%	40%
Teaching values	40%	8%	52%
All six areas	12%	0.3%	4%

Source: "Family in America" survey conducted in February 1992 by the Barna Research Group, Ltd. These data reflect the answers of 519 parents with children under the age of 18.

while the other worked full-time, even though that would mean sacrificing the lifestyle they desired. Sixty-five percent indicated that sacrificing
some of life's pleasures in order to have one parent care for the children
was the preferred option.[12]

Adults were also asked if it would be better to place those
children in a full-time child care program or to have a relative, such as
a grandparent, move in with the family to care for the children while
both parents are at work. Once again, adults overwhelmingly selected
the in-home option; 71 percent preferred to have the relative move in;
22 percent felt the child-care program was a better choice.[13]

SHARING THE LOAD

Despite our culture's emphasis on sexual equality, it is still the mother
who retains most of the obligation for bringing up the children. In one
of our studies on the family, we asked a large sample of parents across
the nation who should bear the responsibility for raising the children.
Ninety-one percent replied that both parents should equally share the
load. But when we asked them what their actual experience has been in
raising the children, we discovered that only 53 percent claim that the
responsibility has been shared equally; nearly as many (43 percent) said
the mother has taken on most of the duties; and just 3 percent claimed
that the father has carried the major burden. And when we quizzed
parents about how (or if) that load gets shared, we found again that the
mother ended up with most of the work.[14]

"If I knew then what I know today, we never would have had
more than one or two kids," sighed Sharon Twarczik, echoing a common
frustration felt by many women. The mother of four kids, she is
disappointed that her husband's promise to share parenting duties
remains unfulfilled. "It's probably the biggest source of conflict we have.
I have to ask him for help everytime I'm struggling. It wasn't supposed
to be this way. We had an agreement before we had Tony [their first
child], but it hasn't panned out."

Of course, husbands see things from a different angle. "I do
the best I can to help her out," was the explanation offered by James
McQuade, a father of three from Mississippi. "But there are just certain

things I need Josie to do. I can't be there all the time, doing everything, like she can. I work eight to ten hours a day, and when I get home, there's not much left in me. I try to spend time with the kids, and to help her however I can, but there has to be a balance in expectations. To be honest, with all the household chores I have to do—mowing the lawn, fixing broken stuff around the house, paying the bills, and so on—I can't be expected to be the parent the kids hang out with the most."

By the admission of parents themselves, mothers are at least twice as likely as fathers to bear the sole responsibility for handling each of six key areas of childrearing. (See Table 5.1 for the data.) In only one of the six areas—teaching values to the children—did at least half of the parents indicate that this was an equally shared endeavor.

Most significant of all, perhaps, was the finding that in 12 percent of the families represented, the mother was responsible for the bulk of the time allocated to all six of the parenting responsibilities we listed. The fathers in the families represented were responsible for the majority of the time committed to those six areas in just three-tenths of 1 percent of the households. And only 4 percent of the families represented had situations in which the mother and father equally shared the responsibility in each of the six parenting responsibilities. These findings point out that even when parents claim (as half do) that the parenting duties are shared equally by the mother and father, the reality may be something far different.

A Gallup survey adds further insight into the sharing of family duties. When asked who was responsible for doing "all or most" of each of nine different common household chores, men dominated only two of the nine areas. Men were identified by 74 percent of the respondents as the most likely spouse to handle minor home repairs, and by 63 percent as the spouse most likely to do yard work. Women, on the other hand, were more likely to do all or most of the laundry (79 percent), care for the children when they are sick (78 percent), care for the children on a daily basis (72 percent), clean the house (69 percent), wash the dishes (68 percent) and pay the bills (65 percent). They were also viewed as the spouse more likely to be the primary discipliner of the children.[15]

Had the question been asked in the surveys, it is possible that the father would have received more credit for the economic burden he bears in providing for the family. Studies typically find that men perceive themselves as contributing to parenting duties more than their wives give them credit for.[16] On balance, it does appear that the typical mother is likely to endure a more-than-equal share of the parenting load.

Moreover, it is likely that men and women have different perceptions of what parenting entails. Women appear to think of "parenting" or "being a good parent" as those activities that relate to their interaction with their children. Men, on the other hand, are more interested in creating an environment in which parenting and family activity can occur. They earn the money, fix the broken equipment, tend to the condition of the house and yard, or champion the maintenance of the cars, thereby allowing the mother to accomplish the more relational, interactive dimension of childraising. Most married adults, it appears, tend to view women as people-managers. Men, whether by design or default, are supposed to manage the infrastructure of the family. Parents can be successful when these two skills work harmoniously.

It is important to point out, though, that despite the anxiety raised over how little energy many fathers devote to parenting, there is little support for the increase of "Mr. Mom" father figures. Among parents, 70 percent said they feel a child under the age of 12 is more likely to grow up happy and content if his or her mother stays at home and cares for the children; only 2 percent feel the children would be better off if Dad stayed home with the kids while Mom worked full-time; 23 percent said it probably would not make any difference.[17]

SPARING THE ROD OR SPOILING THE CHILD?

Most parents think they are doing a pretty good job of disciplining their children. Sixty-two percent believe that they are on-target when it comes to discipline; 12 percent say they are probably too strict; 25 percent claim that they are not strict enough.[18]

But those same people have a harsher assessment of how well other parents keep their children in line: eighty-one percent say that other parents are not strict enough.[19] The thoughts of Alice Breslin, whose children are now grown and raising their own children, reflect those of many parents. "I get tired of going shopping and having to endure the rude and inconsiderate behavior of other people's kids. Sure, kids deserve a bit of slack, and I'm happy to give it to them. But there's no excuse for so much of the bad behavior that you see kids pull in stores and other public places. I would never have let my kids get away with that."

When it comes to disciplining children, two-thirds of all adults approve of spanking children.[20] But, again, there is a big difference between what parents approve of and what they actually do in the course of parenting. Half of all parents do not spank their children; many of those who do spank do so infrequently, "once every few months" or less often. Thus, while a considerable majority approve of spanking as a disciplinary measure in the raising of children, less than three out of ten parents actually do so at least once a month.[21]

For a variety of reasons, today's parents are reluctant to resort to more stringent forms of discipline. Parents fear that harsh punishment will wound a child's self-esteem and lead others to accuse them of child abuse. They also put faith in the advice of medical professionals who advise disciplining without physical contact. Indeed, nearly half of all adults now believe that if a child is allowed to talk back to his or her parents and no disciplinary action is taken, the children will probably not lose respect for the parents.[22] This softer approach to discipline is increasingly accepted in America.

QUANTITY TIME, QUALITY TIME

Few analysts disagree that parents spend too little time with their children. "Kids need intimate interaction with their parents. Ten minutes of superficial conversation around the dinner table won't do it," noted a family counselor in Minneapolis. "If our parents devoted the same amount of time to their children as they do to some of their hobbies and shopping, today's kids would be a transformed generation," said another counselor.

Unexpectedly, even a majority of parents agree. A national survey by Barna Research uncovered the fact that three out of four adults (including 71 percent of all parents) contend that "to raise a child properly, a parent must spend a lot of time with each child, every day." Yet, more than 82 percent of adults agree that "parents today don't spend enough time with their children."[23] Parents do acknowledge the necessity of devoting time to their children and show a willingness to do so. Surveys show that a majority of parents admit that they do not get to spend as much time with their children as they would like to.[24] Apparently, other pressures and priorities intrude in people's lives that take precedence over parenting.

Children today do not receive enough time to develop strong relationships with their parents.

The estimates of the amount of time that parents spend parenting varies. Our research, conducted among teenagers, found that in homes where the mother lived with the child, teens said their mothers spent an average of fifty minutes per week in meaningful interaction with them. In homes where the father lived with the child, teen respondents stated that the father spent fifteen minutes per week in significant involvement with the teen. Although the survey allowed the teenager to define what "significant involvement" meant, there can be little debate that children today do not receive enough time to develop strong relationships with their parents. It is estimated that a century ago parents spent about 54 percent of their waking, married hours in activity related to raising the children. Today, the estimate is just 18 percent.[25]

The usual defense offered by parents is that "it is not the amount of time we spend together that matters as much as the quality of that time." In fact, our survey revealed that 82 percent of adults and 83 percent of parents agree that "it is more important that a parent spend quality time with a child than to spend a lot of time with the child." "My kids don't keep a stopwatch by their side and measure how many hours I spend with them," declared Jack Atkinson. A resident of Ohio, he has two kids and serves as the Little League manager of his son's baseball team. "They want to know that I love them, I will take care of them, and that when they need me I'll be there. And that's my promise to them. To simply promise that they'll get a specific number of hours per week is meaningless. They need a commitment from my heart, not my calendar."

There is no research, however, that supports the view that the quality of the time parents and their offspring spend together is an acceptable substitute for the quantity of time committed to that relationship. Most studies have indicated that the quality-time/quantity-time debate is ill-founded; the issue is not truly an "either/or" choice, but a "both/and" proposition. The children that grow up best adjusted and happiest in life are those whose parents spent considerable amounts of quality time with them. (See Table 5.2 for a survey of activities that parents commonly share with their children.)

SINGLE PARENTS

With the rise in divorce and the increasing proliferation of unwed mothers, there are more single parents in America than ever before—and more in America than in any other industrialized nation.[26] Presently, there are more than 14 million single-parent families in America. That represents more than one out of every seven families in the nation, an increase of 36 percent since 1970.[27] The far-reaching impact of this growth is demonstrated by a Census Bureau estimate that more than six out of every ten children born in the mid-nineties will live in a single-parent home before they reach their eighteenth birthday.

The explosion in the number of single-parent families has not lessened the widespread conviction that raising a child in a single-parent home may have lasting negative effects on the children. It is not unusual, for instance, for single parents to cohabit with a series of partners. Our research shows that 40 percent of all adults agree that "it is not fair to a child to be raised in a household in which his or her parents are not married and in which both parents are living in that home." Yet, these types of households are rapidly increasing.

Single parents are quite different from the typical married-couple parent. Those who go it alone tend to be younger, less educated, and have lower income levels. They face greater difficulty in finding employment that provides stable hours and good pay and often accept jobs that are less time demanding (and, consequently, less financially rewarding).[28]

The parent who usually bears the responsibility for raising the children in a single-parent home is the mother. Although the occurrence of single-parent families headed by a father is growing at a faster rate, that growth is deceptive: in absolute numbers, very few men have custody of their children. A woman is the parent in 86 percent of all single-parent families. That means that for every single-parent family headed by a father, there are six headed by a mother.[29] (Table 5.3 demonstrates the changing demographics of households in America.)

The ratio is even more unbalanced in the minority communities. Among black, single-parent families (which, by the way, actually represent the majority of all black families—61 percent in 1990!), women were the head in 92 percent of those families. Among Hispanics, women headed up 88 percent of single-parent families. Among whites, the figure was 82 percent.[30]

The difficulties of being a single parent are enormous, especially when the parent has gone through a divorce. The emotional trauma caused by loneliness and, in the case of a divorce, by the disharmony in the marriage is considerable. Single parents also feel the burden of balancing many tasks: being a parent, sole financial provider, caretaker of the home, social life coordinator, participant in the church, and community member. It's tough enough trying to handle these tasks when there are two adults in the home; attempting to do it alone is a major cause of stress and health problems.

Despite the economic gains that women have achieved in the past two decades, their earnings still lag behind those of their male counterparts. Family responsibilities tend to exaggerate this problem for single mothers. The median annual income in 1990 for married-couple families was $39,895. Among single-parent families headed by a woman, the median was just $16,932. The picture is even bleaker among single-parent families headed by black or Hispanic women. The average annual incomes in those households were $12,125 and $11,914 respectively.[31] The poverty rate among single-parent families headed by women is six

TABLE
5.2 **Family Activities of the Past Week**

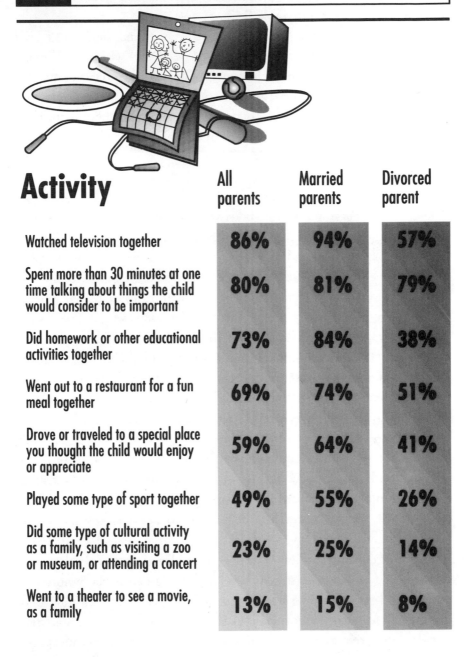

Activity	All parents	Married parents	Divorced parent
Watched television together	86%	94%	57%
Spent more than 30 minutes at one time talking about things the child would consider to be important	80%	81%	79%
Did homework or other educational activities together	73%	84%	38%
Went out to a restaurant for a fun meal together	69%	74%	51%
Drove or traveled to a special place you thought the child would enjoy or appreciate	59%	64%	41%
Played some type of sport together	49%	55%	26%
Did some type of cultural activity as a family, such as visiting a zoo or museum, or attending a concert	23%	25%	14%
Went to a theater to see a movie, as a family	13%	15%	8%

Source: "Family in America" survey conducted in February 1992 by the Barna Research Group, Ltd. These data reflect the answers of 371 parents of children under 18 living in their home.

times higher than that among married-couple families. (The contrast in income levels is shown in Table 5.4.)

Alimony is not the solution to the economic challenges facing most single mothers. Six out of ten divorced adults who seek alimony are granted those payments by the courts. The records indicate, however, that only half of the parents entitled to alimony actually receive the full amount due them. The average child support payment amounts to about $58 per week—in other words, less than $3000 per year.[32]

KIDS PAY A HIGH PRICE

We hear much about the pain and troubles of adults who go through divorce. The emerging research, however, indicates that the people who suffer the most are often the children from those shattered families.

The toll exacted on the children of divorce is often devastating. After the first five years of the divorce, more than one-third of those children (most of whom have spent that entire time in a single-parent home) were significantly worse off for the experience. They were clinically depressed, performed worse in school, had trouble establishing meaningful friendships, exhibited chronic responses to the resulting loneliness and feelings of rejection, and had unrealistic hopes of parental reconciliation.[33] Another study concluded that children from single-parent homes were "consistently shown to be at a disadvantage." They were more prone to suffer from financial hardships; to lack socialization skills both within and outside the home, within the community, and in relationships with the extended family; and to have more difficulty recalling and using information about their world effectively.[34]

"I think we are just beginning to see the results of the devastation we sowed over the last twenty-five years," predicted a professor of cultural studies. "The deep scars laced on our children as a consequence of a narcissistic, driven way of life cannot be ignored or downplayed. For years to come, you will see the ramifications of a divorce-happy, single-parent society when you look at crime statistics, suicide rates, relational crises, moral ambiguity, and the widespread problems of self-esteem that manifest themselves in a myriad of public and private ways."

TABLE 5.3 Household Configurations in America

Type of household	Percentage of households in		
	1970	**1980**	**1991**
All family households	81%	74%	70%
All family households without children	36%	35%	36%
All family households with children	45%	38%	34%
All married-couple family households	71%	61%	55%
Married-couple family households without children under 18	30%	30%	29%
Married-couple family households with children under 18	40%	31%	26%
Single-parent family with male head of household	2%	2%	3%
Single-parent family with female head of household	9%	11%	12%
Male living alone	6%	9%	10%
Female living alone	12%	14%	15%
Other types of households	1%	3%	5%

Source: "Household and Family Characteristics: March, 1991," U.S. Dept. of Commerce, Bureau of the Census, Series P–20, #458.

How serious is the harm resulting from single-parent families? It may be one of the most important conditions threatening not only the family in America, but the well-being of the entire nation. Our studies have consistently pointed out that single parents struggle with a greater range and depth of difficulties than do married adults. They have a diminished sense of joy in life, are less excited about their parenting and family life, and feel neglected by all social institutions: government, churches, employers, family, medical facilities, and so on. Their children face unattractive odds for living healthy, happy, fulfilling lives. Nevertheless, the depressing truth is that the growth of single-parent families is expected to climb over the coming decade.

IS IT ALL WORTH IT?

Is parenting worth the risks and challenges it brings? Despite the struggles and frustrations of raising kids, three out of four parents assert that having children had strengthened their marriage; only 3 percent feel that having children had weakened their marriage.[35] But do the benefits outweigh the costs? When parents were asked to evaluate the totality of their parenting experience and determine the relative balance of their joys and frustrations with their children, the answer was unequivocally in favor of having and raising children. Eighty-nine percent of all parents say that having children has increased their enjoyment of life. Even 84 percent of all single parents conceded that the hardships had been more than compensated for by the enjoyment received.[36] In fact, when the Roper Organization asked women what was the best part of being a woman today, the top answer, given by 60 percent of those interviewed, was motherhood.[37] Clearly, those who ought to know best—parents—heartily endorse the adventure of raising children.

HOW CHRISTIANS CAN RESPOND

Although it sounds trite, the truth remains that America's future is in the hands of its parents. The importance we attach to parenting, the tangible support we provide to parents in their vital task of nurturing young people, and the success parents experience in bringing up their youngsters will greatly influence the destiny of our nation.

| TABLE **5.4** | **Family and Finances** |

Family type   **Annual income**

All families

 **$35,353**

Married-couple families

 **$39,895**

Single-parent families with female head

 **$29,046**

Single-parent families with black female head

$12,125

Single-parent families with Hispanic female head

 **$11,914**

Source: U.S. Bureau of the Census.

In the years ahead, we should expect that families will make greater use of child-care services. We might also expect to see more companies offer on-site or near-site company-sponsored child care, providing parents with visitation privileges during the workday. It is also likely that we will see the passage of legislation standardizing the quality of child care required from providers.

The trend toward small families will continue during the decade. Even immigrant families, as they become acculturated, will have fewer children than did their ancestors. It is feasible that more Baby Busters will opt for childless households.

Expect state and local governments to renew their verbal commitment to crack down on adults who fail to make their alimony payments. Some of this commitment may end up being empty political rhetoric, however, since declining government budgets will limit how much energy and funding governments can put into tracking down deadbeat dads.

We will continue to see increasing numbers of fathers who gain custody of the children in the wake of a divorce. We will not, however, reach a point at which single fathers achieve parity with single mothers. Our society's perception that a mother is better at raising and nurturing the family has remained basically the same, despite the prevailing cultural attitude that tends to minimize the differences between the sexes.

We will also be exposed to more research and public debate over the effects of single-parent households upon children. Whether or not such research will ultimately reawaken the public's appreciation for the importance of marriage and of two-parent households will to a substantial extent depend upon how the media regard and report this information.

Individuals who are considering becoming parents, as well as those who already are parents, would be well-served by thinking through their responsibilities and learning what characteristics tend to make for the healthiest children. By transmitting wholesome values, providing consistent and fair discipline, and creating in the child a sense of accountability for his or her behavior, a parent can instill in each child a strong, loving character.

The Bible offers much wisdom to parents. Making the family Christ-centered, rather than parent- or child-centered, will strengthen personal relationships and build healthy self-images in the children. Lean on God's Word as you strive to achieve a balance between love and discipline. And as you think about your relationships with your children, keep in mind that the amount and quality of the time you spend with them will influence the depth of your relationship with them. Establish positive, predictable habits of communicating with them and involve yourself in their lives. Trying to see the world through a child's eyes can also improve how you relate to him or her.

Parenting ought to be supported in many ways through your church. Determine if your congregation needs to offer programs, classes, or seminars that will give sound, godly advice to new parents. Talk to other parents about the ways the church can help single parents or married couples who are struggling with family conflict. Finally, plan church activities that encourage family togetherness and fun.

Notes

1. *Statistical Abstract of the United States, 1991* (Washington, D.C.: U.S. Dept. of Commerce, Bureau of the Census, 1991), table 67, p. 51.

2. See George Barna, *The Invisible Generation: Baby Busters* (Glendale, Calif.: Barna Research Group, 1992).

3. Based on a nationwide, in-person survey of 1,372 adults conducted in 1990 by National Opinion Research Center of Chicago.

4. From the "Family in America" survey, conducted in February 1992 by the Barna Research Group, Ltd. Also drawn from George Barna, *The Church Today: Insightful Statistics and Commentary* (Glendale, Calif.: Barna Research Group, 1991).

5. Taken from "Roper's America," *Marketing Week* (11 November 1991), 10.

6. Based upon research conducted in 1990 by the Gallup Organization, 100 Palmer Square, Princeton, NJ, 08542.

7. "Family in America" survey, Barna Research Group.

8. Based on a March 1992 interview with Dr. George Gerbner, Professor of Communications at the University of Pennsylvania. Dr. Gerbner has conducted numerous studies on television and its impact on our culture. His work has appeared in numerous journal articles.

9. Lewis Coser et al., *Introduction to Sociology*, 2d ed. (San Diego: Harcourt Brace Jovanovich, 1987), 336.

10. These data were provided by the Census Bureau.

11. "Family in America" survey, Barna Research Group.

12. Ibid.

13. Ibid. A related development of our times is the growing number of grandparents who are taking full responsibility for raising their grandchildren. Currently, there are close to 4 million children who are living with and being raised by their grandparents. These are usually situations in which the grandparent becomes a parent unexpectedly when their own children become incapable of raising the youngsters due to physical or mental illness, abandonment, abuse, or even death. See, for instance, "When Grandma Becomes Mom," *State Register-Journal* (Springfield, Illinois), 23 October 1992, 6-A.

14. "Family in America" survey, Barna Research Group.

15. Gallup Organization poll conducted February 1990. Sample size was 1,234 individuals.

16. Ibid. and "Family in America" survey, Barna Research Group.

17. "Family in America" survey, Barna Research Group.

18. General Social Survey, National Opinion Research Corporation, 1990, consisting of 1,372 nationwide, in-person interviews.

19. Gallup Poll national telephone survey of 1,239 adults, conducted June 1990.

20. Ibid.

21. Ibid.

22. General Social Survey, National Opinion Research Corporation, 1990.

23. "Family in America" survey, Barna Research Group.

24. NBC News telephone survey conducted among 1,555 adults in July 1990.

25. Arlene Skolnick and Jerome Skolnick, *Families in Transition*, 6th ed. (Glenview, Ill: Scott, Foresman & Company, 1989), 15.

26. "Children's Well-Being: An International Comparison," Bureau of the Census, SB/91-1, January 1991.

27. "Household and Family Characteristics: March 1991," U.S. Dept. of Commerce, Bureau of the Census, Series P-20, #458; and "Money Income of Households, Families and Persons in the U.S.: 1990," U.S. Dept. of Commerce, Bureau of the Census, Current Population Reports, series P-60, #174, August 1991.

28. "Single Parents and Their Children," Bureau of the Census, SB-3-89, issued November 1989.

29. Ibid.

30. "Family Demographics," *Public Perspective* (March-April 1991): 93–95.

31. "Money Income of Households, Families and Persons in the U.S.: 1990," in Current Population Reports.

32. Steven Waldman, "Deadbeat Dads," *Newsweek* (4 May 1992), 46–48. Also, "Who's Helping Out," U.S. Dept. of Commerce, Bureau of the Census, Current Population Reports, series P-70, #28, 1988.

33. Judith Wallerstein and Sandra Blakeslee, *Second Chances* (New York: Ticknor & Fields, 1989), xvii.

34. Based on research conducted by researchers at the University of Wisconsin-Madison, reported in paper number #48 of their National Survey of Families and Households series.

35. "Family in America" survey, Barna Research Group.

36. Ibid.

37. This Roper survey was conducted in 1988 and reported in the March 1988 issue of the *Ladies Home Journal.*

CHAPTER SIX

SINGLE AND NEVER BEEN MARRIED

Warren Brewster is twenty-nine years old. He has been dating women since he was in his early teens, but has consistently avoided marriage. Not that he isn't interested: "Sure, I plan to get married when I meet the right person and when the timing is right." After a while of living on his own—including a year-long interlude with a woman who eventually bore his child—Warren has moved back in with his parents. He works full-time as a shipping clerk but does not make much money. "Probably not enough to get a marriage off to a strong start. In time, that'll change. I'll be promoted in the next year or so, and that will raise my salary." He is in no hurry to change his lifestyle. "What's to hurry for? They say you can't hurry love. I've known a lot of women, and plan to have a family, but I just don't think the time is right."

Next time you're in a shopping mall, take a good look at the people hurrying past you. Chances are good that nearly half of them are single adults, and that nearly one out of every four of the adults in your line of sight have never been married. Currently, there are more than

40 million adults in America who have never been married. Although the singles population in our nation comprises three distinct groups, namely, the widowed, the divorced, and those who have never been married, it is the increase of the last group that is primarily responsible for the explosion of the singles market in America.

Those who have never been married make up 60 percent of all single adults. In fact, the proportion of adults who had never been married increased by nearly 40 percent during the two-decade span between 1970 and 1990. By comparison, the proportion of adults who were divorced at the time of the 1990 Census was no different than had been true twenty years earlier, at the time of the 1970 Census. The proportion of adults who had been widowed had increased substantially, but in absolute numbers this group remained the smallest among the three singles subgroups.

Why such a sizeable increase? Investigating the attitudes and behavior of those who have never been married turns up several significant trends:

- more of these people are living with their parents until later ages in life
- increasing numbers of them are having children without getting married
- cohabitation is gaining popularity as a lifestyle option
- those who do get married (and most of them eventually do) are making that commitment at a later age
- sexual activity is commonplace among unmarried people

The nineties promises to be a pivotal time for those who have never been married. They may be the group most likely to feel the confusion caused by our inconsistent cultural values about marriage. On the one hand, they have heard parents, authority figures, and peers proclaim the value of marriage. On the other hand, they have seen how hypocritical behavior and the pressures that marriage places on people can easily destroy the bonds of matrimony. They know too that our culture condones divorce and alternative lifestyles when the marriage proves difficult or just inconvenient.

THE DEMOGRAPHIC PICTURE

Among all adults who are eighteen or older, only one out of four has never been married. "Say what you will about alternative lifestyles," remarked one sociologist, "but the fact remains that Americans are a marrying people. We dabble in alternative forms of family, but when it gets right down to it, we usually fall into a predictable, traditional pattern. The fact that we do so at different ages today than a century ago is less indicative of a perceptual shift regarding family than it is a reflection of the changing life stages of today's population."

Nevertheless, it is perhaps significant that the proportion of adults who have never wedded has been slowly rising for the last twenty-five years. In the late sixties, only 15 percent had not been married; by 1980 the figure was 20 percent; in 1991, it had reached 23 percent.[1]

The never-married group tends to be younger than most adults and to have a lower annual income. Men are more likely than women to belong to the never-married category. In fact, the data show that "old maids" are relatively uncommon. Among all women forty-five or older, just under 5 percent have never been married. In fact, it is just as common for older men never to have been wed (6 percent).[2]

Making ends meet is much more difficult for a single adult than for those who are part of a married-couple household. This is partly attributable to the fact that many of those who have never been married are young adults just getting established in a career. The presence of dual-income households among married couples also makes the monetary comparison considerably more lopsided.

Among single adults who are eighteen or older and have never been married, the average annual income is $10,891. Compare that to the average earnings of married couples ($39,895), divorced individuals ($17,850), and widowed adults ($9,947). Even when college-aged singles are removed from consideration, millions of the never-married who are finished with their full-time schooling have income levels that teeter on the brink of financial insolvency.[3]

BACK TO THE NEST

One of the more intriguing patterns of recent years is that of never-married adults abandoning their independence to move in with their parents. This event tends to occur when these adults are in their middle or late twenties. "It's even hard for me to believe I did this. Ten years ago, my goal in life was to get out from under my parents' roof and have my own life. No rules, no punishments for coming home late, no prohibitions on drinking, no nagging about who my friends are. Today," sighed one twenty-seven-year-old male who returned home a year earlier, "I figure it's a good way to save money, a good way to get to know my parents better, and a decent place to live. I'll have plenty of time later on to flex my freedom."

While singles who move in with their parents represent a small proportion of the total population . . . this lifestyle preference is growing quickly.

What's behind this unusual movement? For some, emotional or personal difficulties or failed relationships have caused them to remain single against their own wishes. Returning to the nest, then, is comforting and reaffirming. Others are drawn back by the high cost of living or perhaps their own relatively low income levels.

While singles who move in with their parents represent a small proportion of the total population (around 15 percent of all adults eighteen or older), this lifestyle preference is growing quickly. In 1970, 47 percent of adults lived with their parents; by 1980, it was virtually unchanged (48 percent). But by 1988, it had risen to 54 percent. The recession of the early nineties helped that figure to climb even further, to an estimated 58 percent in 1992.[4] The decision of these "late nesters" to remain in their parents' homes for an extended period points out the tendency today of many young people to delay their growing up.

A YOUTHFUL VIEW OF LIFE

When discussing the values and attitudes of the never-married group, it is impossible to discount their youth. (The median age of the never-been-married segment is twenty-one.) Maturity and life experiences shape character and values; perhaps lack of maturity helps to explain differences between the never-marrieds, the marrieds, and the divorced.

The never-been-married usually hold values that set them apart from these other groups. For instance, nine out of ten consider family to be very important, but it is no more important to them than having good health. In fact, the never-marrieds are the only group to rate anything else as important as family. They are also more likely than married adults to describe money, a comfortable life, good career, and their time as highly important. (Table 6.1 shows the contrasting values of the never-been-married group.) Furthermore, this group is less likely to cite religion, the Bible, and their community as being very important in their life.[5]

The responses of Candice Palliver, a twenty-four-year-old accountant from West Virginia, typify the views of many of her never-married peers. "I sweated through my academic program so that I could enjoy a life that was meaningful to me, not pleasing to a past generation. I have a great apartment, a nice sports car, and invest my time in a variety of relationships and cultural experiences." She also spends ninety minutes every day at a local health club and is a hard-working volunteer member of a professional association. Unlike her parents, who attended church services every week, she sleeps in on Sunday mornings. "Religion is for those who can't piece life together. My education taught me that I can make life be what I want it to be, if I work hard enough and have goals I'm striving to meet. I love my family, but I can't let them hold me back from what I am capable of accomplishing."

Never-married singles also tend to hold more liberal views on current issues. For instance, they are less likely to believe that abortion is morally wrong; to contend that today's music has a negative influence on people's lives; to describe themselves as conservative; and to say that if the traditional family unit falls apart American society will collapse. By the same token, they are more likely than currently married adults to believe that the moral and ethical standards of Americans are as high as ever; to define freedom as meaning you can do anything you want to do; to say that it is very unlikely for a man and woman to have a deep, lasting friendship that does not turn into a sexual relationship; and to suggest that everything in life is negotiable.[6]

Fewer never-marrieds describe themselves as religious. Compared to married adults, who consider religion to be among the more important elements in their lives, the never-married see religion as only a moderately important influence in their lives. Never-married individuals are only half as likely as married adults to categorize themselves as born-again Christians. They are less likely than currently or previously married people to believe that the Bible's teachings are totally accurate; that Jesus Christ rose from the dead and is alive today; that they have a responsibility to share their religious beliefs with other people; and that there is a God who hears people's prayers and has the power to answer them.[7] This group is also less likely to attend church services, to read the Bible, to attend religious education classes at a church, or to pray.

"I feel very blessed to be in a church that can afford to have a pastor for our singles," noted a minister of a mainline Protestant church in the Midwest. "As a married adult with grown children, I don't relate very well to the worldview of today's young singles. They are probably no more rebellious than the single adults of my own day, but they seem more hardened in their attitudes about Christ and in their dealings with each other. They have an edge that I cannot seem to get past. Reaching them with truth and hope and the values espoused by the church takes a very special gift."

Twelve percent of the aggregate adult population can be described as evangelical Christian, but when that categorization is broken down, we find it fits 13 percent of the married adults, 10 percent of the never marrieds, 8 percent of the divorced, and 16 percent of the widowed.[8] This finding is surprising because it suggests that those who have not been married are just as likely as the presently married to qualify as evangelicals, even though the never-marrieds are clearly a less religious group and are much less likely to hold to orthodox religious beliefs. The conclusion we can infer is that the never-marrieds are either

TABLE
6.1 How Never-Been-Marrieds Are Different

Opinion	Never Married	Currently Married	Currently Divorced
The moral and ethical standards of Americans are as high today as ever.	31%	18%	23%
If the traditional family unit falls apart, American society will collapse.	60%	76%	67%
Freedom means being able to do whatever you want to do.	48%	36%	36%
Today's popular music has a negative influence on most people.	16%	33%	19%
Abortion is morally wrong.	33%	52%	33%
It is very unlikely for a man and a woman to have a deep, lasting friendship without it becoming a sexual relationship.	37%	22%	39%
Everything in life is negotiable.	63%	45%	53%

Source: "OmniPoll" studies conducted in 1991-92 by the Barna Research Group, Ltd.

strongly committed to their religious faith or generally ignore it altogether.

Never-marrieds also share some distinctive family perspectives. Never-been-married adults possess a cautiousness about people and relationships that explains, in part, why they are remaining single until later in life. For instance, they are less than half as likely as married and divorced adults to want to return to traditional family values, but instead prefer the creation of a new values system. "You can't go backwards in time," declared Joyce Norberg, a systems analyst in her early thirties. "We can probably learn some useful things from what our parents' generation experienced, but their ways won't work today. We'll have to create our own responses to a world that reinvents itself every few years."

Cynicism about marriage also characterizes never-married adults. They are nearly twice as likely as married adults (but somewhat less likely than divorced adults) to believe that anyone getting married these days should expect to eventually get divorced. This is closely related to their view that you really can't trust anyone other than family and close friends these days. Such outlooks help explain why this group tends to delay marriage. It also sheds light on why they are three times more likely than married adults to say that they are lonely.[9]

To summarize, people who have yet to walk down the aisle tend to be more focused on establishing a comfortable and prosperous lifestyle; are less likely to turn to religion for guidance or support; are more likely than other groups to be skeptical about people and relationships, including the durability of traditional family systems; and possess more liberal views on political and social matters and issues of personal morality.

IS MARRIAGE ON THE HORIZON?

Don't let the label "never been married" fool you: most of these adults are seeking the right opportunity to get married. More than eight out of ten never-been-married singles say that they will either definitely get married (38 percent) or would like to get married (45 percent). A relatively small contingent says that they are not very interested in being married (9 percent) or that they definitely will not get married (5 percent).[10]

The reasons these singles seek to become married has changed markedly over the years. Instead of searching for a permanent, loving, relationship and the opportunity to raise children, today's never-married adults are more interested in long-term companionship.[11] The turmoil of witnessing firsthand marital conflict and divorce has left never-married singles gun-shy about marriage. They still believe in the concept and look forward to having their own family. But instead of boldly proclaiming that they are looking for the right person with whom they can spend the rest of their lives, they often settle for someone with whom they can establish a close, warm, satisfying, long-term friendship. In such a relationship, love is desirable but not necessarily expected. (Table 6.2 provides more details on what this group wants from marriage.)

Sadly, millions of never-married adults believe that finding a lifelong love relationship is unlikely in the nineties. Although they want partners who treasure enduring relationships, the never-married dismiss these expectations as impractical. "You don't want to get your hopes up," explained one woman who is initiating what she hopes will be a long-term relationship. "If you set your sights too high," warned a single male in his late twenties, "you'll just get disappointed. It's not like it used to be." Instead, they set their sights upon coupling with a compatible, caring individual who will provide intimacy, if not true, lasting love.

Most older, married adults, look down on the never-marrieds' willingness to settle for mere friendship as the basis for selecting a spouse. For most singles who want to get married, this is neither a choice nor a compromise; it is contemporary reality, the only viable option in a marriage-hostile culture. Life, in their eyes, is a series of trade-offs, and settling for close companionship is better than remaining lonely.

SINGLES AND SEX

Since the last decade, more adults have come to reject the idea that sexual activity should be confined to marriage. Most single adults in America now believe that as long as you "love" or "care for" another person, sexual intercourse is a natural and permissible part of the relationship.[12] Most adults who have yet to experience marriage have no hesitation about experiencing premarital sexual intimacy. Most never-married adults lose their virginity early in their youth and are likely to have experienced sex with several partners by the time they find a mate.[13]

Overall, most of today's adults view marriage as a means of personal fulfillment, not as a cultural obligation. If a marriage promises to provide the relational comfort and support required by the individual, then it is an attractive option. Otherwise, marriage is perceived as a liability.

Young, never-married adults are surprisingly open about their sexual values. "My parents would die if they knew I was telling people this," one young woman from the South declared. "I probably sleep with one or two guys a week. I'm careful because of AIDS and other diseases, but the quality of men I date would not put me at risk. Anyway, I'm not a slut just because I have sex with a lot of people. It's the way we live today. None of us are desperate about marriage." Her parents, who are involved in a local Christian church, have told her that they disapprove strongly of her peers' lifestyle. Still, they have no idea how "rich" her sex life is. She continued, "Some day I'll settle down and have a family and all, but for now, people like me have to take care of our needs. Worrying about virginity is a joke. I went to a public high school with a class of about four hundred. Of the two hundred girls I graduated with, maybe 10 percent of them hadn't done it with someone by the time they left school. When I get married, I know the guy I settle down with will have had other encounters, and so will I. But our commitment will be to each other."

Although most of these individuals will eventually tie the knot, they are getting married later in life. (The average age of a person's first marriage these days is 26 for men, 24 for women.) According to these singles, the main reasons for their casual pursuit of marriage are related to personal finances (namely, the difficulties of getting a job, paying off school loans, and saving money in preparation for marriage), the nature of personal relationships today (they have greater difficulty meeting like-minded people and finding an appropriate partner), fear of

TABLE
6.2

Why Never-Been-Marrieds Want to Get Married

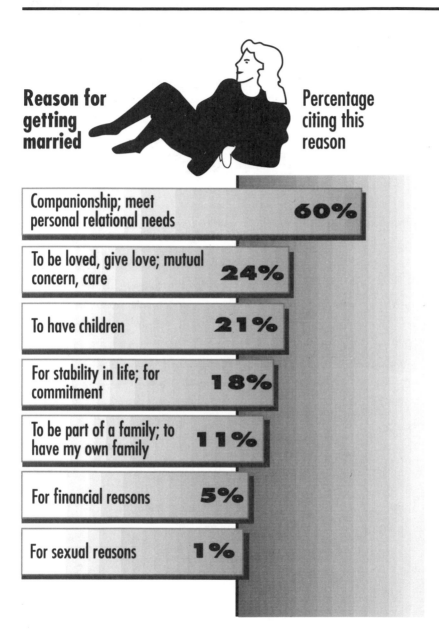

Reason for getting married

Percentage citing this reason

Companionship; meet personal relational needs	**60%**
To be loved, give love; mutual concern, care	**24%**
To have children	**21%**
For stability in life; for commitment	**18%**
To be part of a family; to have my own family	**11%**
For financial reasons	**5%**
For sexual reasons	**1%**

Source: "Family in America" survey conducted in February 1992 by the Barna Research Group, Ltd. These data reflect the views of the 206 adults in the study who had never been married. The percentages exceed 100 percent because each person was allowed to give multiple answers.

divorce (a fear, however, that seems to dissipate as an individual ages and faces the less appealing alternative of remaining unattached), and the widespread acceptance of sexual experimentation and bearing children outside of marriage, rendering marriage a less urgent necessity.[14]

Where do single adults go to meet prospective mates today? Here, again, we see important differences from previous years. A study conducted ten years ago determined that singles relied most heavily upon friends for introductions to other singles; on bars and clubs; and on parties and other social gatherings.[15] Today, the most popular spots for meeting other singles and finding a partner are work, school, and church. Social and exercise clubs have lost their allure to most singles; similarly, the "meat market" reputation of singles bars and nightclubs has repelled many adults who are not married.[16]

Those who have never wed show surprisingly little difference from their elders in the way they regard marriage. Their views on marriage are unexpectedly traditional, more so than their views on most lifestyle issues. Most of them believe that marriage is an idea that is reasonable and fits our culture (85 percent). Even though they are more accepting than their elders of cohabitation and divorce, a majority of them (57 percent) say that marriage is necessary for family stability.[17]

Even though most of them harbor concerns about the future of marriage, they also possess traditional hopes about husband-wife relationships. Seventy percent of the never-married crowd say marriage should be thought of as a permanent arrangement between the people involved, and 75 percent believe that God intended for the partners to remain married for life. Three out of four reject the idea that it is better to remain single for life than to get married.[18]

These adults are not so skeptical as to be hardened against the traditions of the past, but they are sufficiently wise in the ways of the world to know that a marriage will face challenges. About one-third of them contend that anyone getting married is likely to wind up divorced. Most of them do not believe that having children will smooth out the rough edges of a marriage. However, most of them are aware that single parenting is an arduous task; six out of ten of them acknowledge that it is more difficult to raise a child as a single parent, and more than half agree with the statement that being raised in a single-parent home puts the child at a disadvantage in life.[19]

Taken in their entirety, these attitudes demonstrate a healthy awareness of, and respect for, marital stresses and hardships. One must hope, though, they also reflect a realistic belief that marriage is a good thing and can work out under the right circumstances.

A NEW STRATEGY FOR SUCCESS

Afraid of being burned in marriage, most of today's never-been-married adults are adopting what they hope will be a marital insurance policy: cohabitation. While six out of ten adults reject cohabitation as a way of determining whether or not a marriage will be successful, nearly the same percentage of these adults say that it is the best way to create a successful partnership.[20]

We can see that never-married adults have truly taken this philosophy to heart. Cohabitation jumped 740 percent between 1970 and 1989, and that growth is showing little evidence of slowing down. From 1987 through 1989, there was an 88 percent increase. Among adults age eighteen to twenty-five, cohabitation skyrocketed by 1,892 percent during that same three year time span—a twenty-fold increase![21]

Until recently, analysts reported that cohabitation was most common among the divorced, blacks, urban residents, and those living in the northeastern and western states.[22] The past five years have seen a broadening of the trend as more and more people have accepted cohabitation as a natural development in a significant relationship. "It's no longer a yuppie thing, or a Boomer behavior, or a strategy among the wary," was the assessment of one professor of sociology. "Living together is now as widely accepted a behavior as driving on the right-hand side of the road, or taking a shower in the morning."

Although journalists have fallen all over themselves to impress us with the awesome proportional increases in cohabitation, their reporting has masked a simple fact: at the moment, just 4 percent of the population that is nineteen or older is living with someone of the opposite sex to whom they are not married. Overall, 17 percent of

American adults have lived together before their first marriage, while only 25 percent have lived with someone of the opposite sex apart from marriage.[23]

A BAD INSURANCE POLICY

Ironically, cohabitation is probably more indicative of Americans' desire to have a strong marriage than of a society that has abandoned all morality. Most people move in with a partner because they intend to get married but want to "make sure" that their prospective mate is the right person. Few people cohabit with the expectation that they will simply "live with" the other person indefinitely. The views of a young woman from California are typical: "We're getting used to each other, learning about each other, and moving closer to a decision. I think—and really hope—we'll get married. But we both agree that marriage is way too important a decision to just jump in without first testing the waters. This has been a real good experience for both of us, and we know we'll be better off for it."

The evidence, however, is overwhelmingly clear that cohabitation as insurance against divorce does not work.

To their credit, most cohabitors not only think of living together as a prelude to marriage, most of them make good on that original intention. About three out of every five couples who move in together for any length of time eventually wed.[24]

The research also suggests that most people who experiment with cohabitation usually limit that choice to someone they would consider marrying. A massive nationwide study of more than 13,000 adults, conducted by researchers at the University of Wisconsin, found that of people who got married for their first time between 1980 and 1987, 44 percent had cohabited with someone prior to their marriage; in 89 percent of those cases, they had cohabited only with their eventual spouse. (It is intriguing to note that among those adults who got married for their second or later time during those same years, 60 percent cohabited prior to their latest marriage; 90 percent of those individuals, too, had lived solely with their mate-to-be after their most recent divorce.)[25]

The evidence, however, is overwhelmingly clear that cohabitation as insurance against divorce does not work. In fact, just the opposite appears to be true: people who cohabit before marriage have a higher likelihood of divorce than do those individuals who marry without having lived together. Studies have shown that cohabitors have an 80 percent greater likelihood of experiencing a marital breakup than do individuals who marry without a period of cooperative living.[26]

WHY COHABITATION FAILS

For two decades, social scientists have suggested that societal constraints have prevented cohabitation from working as a preparatory step for marriage. The argument, which seemed sensible but was not supported by hard data, was that traditional views on marriage excluded cohabitation as a legitimate premarital ritual. In a society whose ethical and moral base was Judeo-Christian, living together without being married was viewed as sinful. Thus, the analysts concluded, society's hostility toward cohabitation effectively doomed any couple who attempted to test their compatibility through a "trial period." Because society looked down on cohabiting couples, the theory went, such people were fighting odds too large to overcome.

But recent studies have provided the insights that were missing for so long. In fact, the fear of social rejection was hardly a factor at all. What the data did show was that individuals who engage in cohabitation were more likely to disagree with other traditional ideas about family and marriage. For instance, a University of Wisconsin study found that cohabitors are more likely than never-been-married adults who have never cohabited to approve of divorce, to approve of premarital sexual intercourse, to be more tolerant of sexual infidelity in a marriage, to have children outside of marriage, to believe that it is acceptable for mothers to work full-time, and to agree that full-time day care is appropriate for young children.[27]

Divorce is more likely among cohabitors who marry, partially because the act of "testing" the relationship amounts to a lack of commitment. Studies among unmarried people who live together revealed they have a higher expectation of divorce than do other couples who marry. They also find that their marriages, when compared to those of the couples who did not cohabit, are characterized by the following attributes:

- they show lower levels of overall marital satisfaction
- they have a lower overall commitment to marriage as an institution
- they are less likely to see their spouse as their best friend
- they are less likely to believe that their spouse respects them
- they have a greater fear of divorce
- they are more restless about their marriage and outside relationships.[28]

The evidence shows that cohabitors have had more sexual partners prior to the marriage than have other adults, weakening the trust and satisfaction in the marriage itself.

One of the most enlightening statistics may be that people who cohabit are more likely to be unfaithful to their spouses after getting married than are those who did not cohabit. This behavior is likely related to their casual regard for marriage. Cohabitors are less likely to see fidelity as important in marriage, are more likely to risk an affair if they have strong reason to believe that their spouse will not find out, and are more likely to describe themselves as sexually attractive or erotic.[29]

Despite cohabitation's poor track record and the continued opposition it receives from conservative religious groups, the practice continues to spread. Most Americans are either accepting of, or ambivalent toward, cohabitation. People who uphold traditional moral values are alarmed most by the rise in cohabitation because they fear it will weaken our esteem of marriage. The most recent information available appears to support their concern. Nevertheless, those who harbor serious reservations about the practice stand in the minority.

BABIES WITHOUT LIVE-IN FATHERS

Another ominous trend that singles have embraced is that of having children outside of marriage. From 1985–1989, 43 percent of all first births to women between the ages of eighteen and twenty-four were to unmarried women, the majority of whom had never been married. This represents a 207 percent increase since the 1960–1964 period, when just 14 percent of all first births to women in that age group were out of wedlock. The pattern of young women bearing children outside of marriage has been steadily increasing. In the early sixties, 14 percent of women ages fifteen to twenty-four who gave birth were not married; this figure jumped to 22 percent in the early seventies, then to 35 percent in the early eighties, and climbed to more than 43 percent in the early nineties.[30]

Women bearing children outside of marriage is not a new development, of course. All of us are familiar with historical and fictitious accounts of "fallen women" whose loose morals resulted in unexpected pregnancies. More recently, in the fifties and sixties, episodes involving unwed mothers appeared on television programs, and in the movies "shotgun weddings" became the standard fare in a number of plots. Script writers could certainly draw from real-life experiences for their inspiration: in the early sixties, among girls fifteen to nineteen years of age, one-half of all children were conceived out of wedlock.[31]

By the late eighties, however, the numbers had risen even more dramatically. Four out of five babies conceived by girls in their teens were out of wedlock. Whereas half of all teen pregnancies in the early sixties resulted in a marriage after conception but before birth, the proportion dropped to less than one out of four by 1989. One young woman stated, "I made one mistake. I'm not gonna multiply it by marrying the guy and ruining what's left of my life."[32]

The shotgun wedding is receding into the past. In fact, these days many single-and-pregnant women have willingly conceived their child without any intention of marrying the father. The social pressure that drove many couples to the altar before the birth of their child is absent in today's culture.

Why do some women want to bear children outside of marriage? Usually, they fear not having the chance to raise a child, but at the same time they do not want to give up their lifestyle and personal freedoms at too young an age or risk the possibility of a divorce. Encouraged in the seventies and eighties by the wider acceptance of the "personal choice lifestyle" ("do whatever you want as long as it does not directly hurt others"), young adults have had comparatively little pressure placed on them to rethink this approach to starting a family. "It's my life, my body, my child. My parents don't understand, and I don't really expect them to. They live in a whole different world than I do," declared a twenty-five-year-old unmarried mother of an infant daughter. "She's a beautiful baby, and I love her. I wanted this child for me, not for my parents, not because of my relationship with the guy who impregnated me. I want to have a child, and I do, and if everyone would stop ragging on me about the decision, things will be just fine."

HOW WE PREPARE PEOPLE FOR MARRIAGE

Most of today's never-been-married adults are under thirty years of age. It is therefore instructive to examine what family values and practices they have absorbed from their parents. Sociologists and psychologists generally agree that such experiences and teaching have a profound impact on the behavior of people as they mature. In many cases, it is possible to predict with a high degree of accuracy the quality of family life an individual is likely to experience, based on what that person has lived through.

Sexual activity has increased by leaps and bounds among young people.

Let's consider, for instance, the prevalent views on sexual morality. In the early seventies, only one out of every four adults felt that premarital intercourse was acceptable; today, about half of the population endorses such behavior. The proportion of adults who claim that premarital sex is "always wrong" has declined to barely one-fourth of the adult population. Most adults who are now in their thirties and forties indicated that not only did they have sexual liaisons when they were young, but also that they do not regret having done so. As you consider these statistics, understand that such views will likely be transmitted to young people and will in turn shape the perspectives held by young adults regarding family life.[33]

Attitudes toward the sexual conduct of teenagers are changing radically, too. Adults are about evenly divided as to whether the public schools should encourage youngsters to use condoms or to abstain from sexual intercourse. Such an even division of opinion is, in itself, a dramatic departure from what might have been anticipated in the past. What may be most revealing is the fact that among the Baby Boomers (those aged twenty-nine to forty-seven in 1993), a majority (51 percent) favored the use of condoms, while among Baby Buster adults (those eighteen to twenty-eight at the time), condom use was preferred over abstinance by almost a four to one margin (69 percent to 19 percent).[34]

Sexual activity has increased by leaps and bounds among young people. In 1970, 5 percent of fifteen-year-olds were sexually active; today, it is close to one-third. Two decades ago, just under half of all nineteen-year-olds were sexually active; today, it is nine out of ten. Fewer than one out of every five adults who gets married for the first time these days is a virgin.[35]

The influence of such attitudes is pervasive. Among adults who have never been married, one out of every four has actively dated another person who was still married at the time. In fact, one out of four never-been-married adults admits to having had sexual relations with another individual who was married at the time.[36] Apart from the moral harm caused by rampant sexual involvement, the health hazards are substantial. In spite of sex-education classes and health warnings offered in the schools, most high school students do not use condoms when they have sex, increasing the possibility of contracting the HIV virus. (It should be added that condoms provide only minimal protection against that disease.) More than one million unintended teenage pregnancies occur each year, half of which are ended by abortion (which is itself an emotionally traumatic experience). Sadly, but not surprisingly, in excess of three million teenagers contract sexually transmitted diseases each year.[37]

New studies of the children of broken families show convincingly that these young adults frequently imitate the behavior they witnessed in their youth—even those practices they disdained. Thus, children from homes with bad marriages are more prone to have negative views about marriage and to regard it with a greater sense of futility. Children who have gone through a divorce are more likely to see their own marriages end in divorce. Young adults whose parents failed to model skills for negotiating conflict, compromising, and effective communication are more likely to show similar limitations in their relationships.[38]

It is clear that the new attitudes toward marriage, sexual activity, and family that have gained the upper hand during the past twenty years have had a decidedly corrupting effect on young adults. As a result, many of them have delayed marriage or have set themselves up for divorce and the attendant misery.

HOW CHRISTIANS CAN RESPOND

Most single adults will marry at some point in their lives. The age at which they first do so will probably top out right about where it is today (twenty-six for men, twenty-four for women). We might expect to see the proportion of adults who never marry to rise slowly and slightly, but no major shifts are likely.

The percentage of the never-married who move in with their parents will probably stay about the same. In the future, some individuals who currently view the care of their aging parents as their responsibility may decide to forsake that obligation and entrust their care to government-sponsored health-care programs.

The frequency of sexual interaction among singles is not likely to change: in fact, given our cultural obsession with sexual and personal freedoms, the remaining barriers to sexual restraint may come under fire. Enemies of marriage may launch an attack on several fronts. The Christian church may well remain the only institution forcefully promoting sexual abstinence. Adults will continue to pay lip service to the need for caution, advocating so-called safe sex, but that will be merely a facade for sex-on-demand with precautions taken to guard against AIDS and other sexually transmitted diseases. Both sexual involvement and cohabitation will remain popular as will the acceptance of nouveau family definitions.

As a Christian, how would you defend God's requirement that people refrain from sexual intercourse before marriage? In a society in which morals have been diluted to mean each individual's personal preferences, someone must be able to stand up for God's truth and articulate His position in a logical, unemotional manner.

We have to be careful to avoid judgmental posturing. Yes, sin is sin. Yet we must show compassion for young people who grow up these days in a moral vacuum and face the hurt of broken families and confusing choices. The church has a major responsibility—and opportunity—to restate the case for the traditional family, committed personal relationships, and responsible sexual behavior. If we can do so in a loving manner, others may be persuaded to abandon cohabitation and premarital sex.

If you are a single person striving to live a godly life, recognize that God's rules are intended to spare you from the consequences of sinful behavior and the pain of broken relationships. If you have friends who belong to the never-been-married category, think through how you would have them consider God's plan for relationships and marriage.

Notes

1. "Singleness in America," U.S. Dept. of Commerce, Bureau of the Census, SB-4-89, November 1989.

2. "Marital Status and Living Arrangements: March 1987," U.S. Dept. of Commerce, Bureau of the Census, Current Population Reports, series P-20, #423, April 1988, table 1.

3. See "Money Income of Households, Families and Person in the United States, 1990," U.S. Dept. of Commerce, Bureau of the Census, Current Population Reports, series P-60, #174, 1991, table 28.

4. "Singleness in America," Bureau of the Census; Barna Research Group estimates; "Household and Family Characteristics: March 1991," U.S. Dept. of Commerce, Bureau of the Census, series P-20, #458, 1992, table 16; and Paula Ries and Anne Stone, eds., *The American Woman, 1992–93* (New York: Norton, 1992), 245.

5. These figures were first reported in George Barna, *The Barna Report, 1992–1993: America Renews Its Search for God* (Ventura, Calif.: Regal, 1992), chapter 1.

6. Data from several national "OmniPoll" telephone surveys conducted in 1991 and 1992 by Barna Research Group, Ltd.

7. From "Omnipoll 2–92," conducted July 1992 by the Barna Research Group, Ltd. See the Note to the Reader at the beginning of this book for the definition of "born-again Christian" used in this survey.

8. From "Omnipoll 1–92," conducted in January 1992 by the Barna Research Group, Ltd. See the Note to the Reader for the definition of "evangelical Christian" used in this survey.

9. These figures come from "Omnipoll 2–91," "Omnipoll 2–92," and the "Family Views and Support" survey (June 1992), all conducted by the Barna Research Group, Ltd.

10. Data from "Family in America" survey, Barna Research Group, Ltd., conducted in February 1992. The national random sample size was 1,009 adults.

11. "Omnipoll 2–92," Barna Research Group.

12. "Family in America" survey, Barna Research Group.

13. Ibid.

14. Ibid.

15. These findings came from a large-scale national survey of single adults, reported in Jacqueline Simenauer and David Carroll, *Singles* (New York: Simon and Schuster, 1982), chapter 1.

16. From "Omnipoll 2–91," Barna Research Group.

17. Based on data from the "Family in America" survey, Barna Research Group.

18. Ibid.

19. Ibid.

20. Ibid.

21. These figures were cited in an article describing a study on family systems by Find/SVP, based on government statistics, published in *Marketing Week* (24 June 1991), 28.

22. A good example is the analysis provided by Oxford Analytica in their massive study of American society. Their work related to family matters is summarized in Oxford Analytica, *America in Perspective* (Boston: Houghton-Mifflin, 1986), 86–99.

23. See Larry Bumpass and James Sweet, "National Estimates of Cohabitation: Cohort Levels and Union Stability," paper #2 in the National Survey of Families and Households, published by the Center for Demography and Ecology, University of Wisconsin-Madison, 18.

24. See James Sweet and Larry Bumpass, "Young Adults' Views of Marriage, Cohabitation, and Family," paper #33 in the National Survey of Families and Households, published by the Center for Demography and Ecology, University of Wisconsin-Madison.

25. See Bumpass and Sweet, "National Estimates of Cohabitation," 19.

26. *Research Alert, Future Vision* (Naperville, Ill.: Sourcebooks Trade, 1991), 43.

27. See Bumpass and Sweet, "Young Adults' Views of Marriage, Cohabitation, and Family," and Elizabeth Thomson and Ugo Colella, "Cohabitation and Marital Stability: Quality or Commitment," paper #23 in the National Survey of Families and

Households, published by the Center for Demography and Ecology, University of Wisconsin-Madison.

28. Bumpass and Sweet, "Young Adults' Views of Marriage, Cohabitation, and Family." See also Andrew Greeley, *Faithful Attraction* (New York: Tor, 1991).

29. Greeley, *Faithful Attraction.*

30. "The Fertility of American Women: June 1990," U.S. Dept. of Commerce, Bureau of the Census, series P-20, #454, October 1991.

31. Ibid.

32. Ibid.

33. Data from 1972 and 1988 were compared from a General Social Survey, NORC; additional data were taken from a survey conducted among Baby Boomers for *Rolling Stone* in 1988 by Peter Hart & Associates.

34. "Family Support and Views" survey, Barna Research Group.

35. Data from the National Center for Health Statistics; "National and International Religion Report" (P.O. Box 21433, Roanoke, VA 24018), 13 January 1992, 8; "Family in America" survey, Barna Research Group; and information provided by the Centers for Disease Control.

36. "Family in America" survey, Barna Research Group.

37. Data from the National Center for Health Statistics; "National and International Religion Report," 13 January 1992, 8; "Family in America" survey, Barna Research Group; Centers for Disease Control.

38. Frances Goldschneider and Linda Waite, *New Families, No Families?* (Berkeley, Calif.: Univ. of California Press, 1991), 21–45.

CHAPTER SEVEN

HOMOSEXUAL FAMILIES

To many Americans, especially older ones, the very notion of two adults of the same sex living together or being married to each other shatters their notion of family. As one elderly gentleman from the Midwest stammered in apparent disgust when the topic was broached in an interview, "I don't know what you call that, I just know it's not right. I've got some names for it, sure, but family is not one of them." In this chapter we will examine one of the most controversial nouveau family groups: homosexual adults who live together.

IS A HOMOSEXUAL COUPLE REALLY A FAMILY?

The traditional Western view defines a family as a group of people headed by a man and a woman who have an emotional, physiological, and legal connection to each other. Part of the Judeo-Christian moral code has been the belief that God declares homosexual relations to be "an abomination"; consequently, most cultures in the Western world have prohibited legally and rejected morally sexual relations between people of the same sex.[1]

In the nineteenth century, England was so forcefully opposed to homosexual acts that the laws against such behavior were unwritten—largely, it is said, because people were too embarrassed to have to explain to Queen Victoria the details of those activities! Until recently, American society, like most other developed nations, has had legal sanctions against those who practiced homosexual relations.

But the times are changing—and quite rapidly when it comes to views about sexual preferences, marriage, and family lifestyles. Many Western nations that formerly had prohibitions against homosexuality have since removed those constraints: England, Canada, France, and Holland are among them. Each of those nations has had periods during which public figures have championed and celebrated gay rights. Generally, these countries have come to pride themselves on protecting or providing true freedom for all people, attitudes, or lifestyles that stray from the norm; they argue that if these lifestyles cause no injury to the public interest, they should enjoy legal protection.

The spirited debate that homosexuality raises today was brought to the fore in this country in the sixties. At that time, America was swept up in a revolution of "sexual enlightenment" that demanded equality of the sexes, freedom to have unique forms of family, and toleration of same-sex relationships. Gradually, the public has come to accept many of those demands.

Many analysts identify a clash between police and homosexuals at a gay bar in New York City in 1969 as a turning point. Until that time, most homosexuals were "closet" gays; their behavior was considered deviant and perverse, and few of them would publicly disclose the fact that they were not heterosexual. But tensions continued to build as homosexuals increasingly sought the freedom to search out their relational needs without fear of legal reprisal. The New York incident catalyzed many homosexuals to go public and take pride in their differences. The media focused greater attention on the issue, and homosexuals became more visible as they formed local and national movements. Policymakers started listening to the demands of a group that previously had been politically inert and legally powerless.[2]

Consequently, many state laws prohibiting homosexual activities were repealed on the grounds that such restrictions hindered a person's freedom of expression or right to privacy. Since Illinois overturned its laws on homosexual prohibitions in the sixties, the last quarter-century has seen most states jump on the bandwagon to throw out laws that have been on the books for nearly two hundred years. Today, a majority of states condone private homosexual activity between consenting adults. Even in states where the laws remain in force, enforcement agencies generally ignore violations.

The late sixties and seventies also saw the medical community become divided on the issue of homosexuality. Some psychologists rejected homosexuality, citing it as a learned behavior that is abnormal, unrelated to genetics, and treatable. Others have countered that homosexuality is not a matter of choice but an innate, natural lifestyle. Medical researchers, without taking sides, have shown that gays do have a higher-than-average probability of contracting a plethora of diseases from their contacts, most notably AIDS and various venereal diseases.

A RIGHT OR A WRONG?

People who study and support the democratic process don't always agree on whether homosexual lifestyles are a right guaranteed by the Constitution. Some say they are: "One of the amazing qualities about our democracy is that every person has the freedom to live how he or she wants, as long as they fall within prescribed parameters of socially acceptable behavior," explained a political scientist who teaches at a state

The homosexual community has maintained a well-funded and well-organized lobbying effort over the past several years.

university. "In contemporary America, perhaps more than any other society that has experimented with democracy, sexual aberrations are not just a means of testing those freedoms, but of wresting from the society some of the nuances of freedom. Personally, I find it disgusting, but legally, allowing such activity is merely consistent with our system."

A professor at a Christian college disagrees: "Gay rights is essentially an oxymoron. Our nation was founded on the belief that God's principles are the basis of our society and our Constitution. One of God's principles is that men and women, under prescribed circumstances, may have the privilege of sexual activity together, but that unisexual behavior is a defilement of the person and abhorrent to God. To suggest that it would be 'puritanical' or 'tyrannical' to outlaw homosexuality is absurd. That argument is a politically correct way of saying that the law ought to have no basis in the Judeo-Christian moral code, which means that we must throw out the entire Constitution and start over with an entirely new worldview. I doubt that most Americans have a carefully conceived view on this, but I also doubt that they'd be willing to exchange the Constitution for a new, radically liberalized blueprint for society."

RECASTING THE HOMOSEXUAL IMAGE
The homosexual community has maintained a well-funded and well-organized lobbying effort over the past several years. To some degree, they have been successful in changing public perceptions of homosexuality. Some of those efforts, and the consequent changes, have included the following:

- Funding an image campaign designed to remove the social stigma of being homosexual and to portray gay adults in a positive light. This has included a determined effort to erase negative terminology used to describe homosexual people and to substitute more neutral and positive terms, such as "gay" and "alternative lifestyle."
- Widely proclaiming that 10 percent of the population is gay, thereby making such lifestyles more common than most people would have imagined.
- Using their own network of media to communicate within the gay community, including gay magazines, newspapers,

and theaters. They have also campaigned successfully for radio and television programs carried on the major networks and their affiliates and for motion pictures that portray homosexuals favorably.

- Developing several powerful lobbying groups that wield considerable influence on legislation pending before Congress and in many state legislatures.

- Challenging religious leaders to disregard (or reinterpret) the biblical view of homosexuality. Many major church groups have bowed to the pressure, including the United Methodist denomination, the Episcopal Church, the Presbyterian Church U.S.A., and other mainline Protestant groups.

The persistence and focused efforts of the gay community have radically transformed the American view of sexuality in less than a quarter of a century. Although the nation is nowhere close to accepting homosexual lifestyles as being on a par with heterosexual relationships, a significant minority of the populace now supports the notion that an adult should follow his or her natural sexual inclinations and establish a home with the individual of his or her choice—regardless of that person's gender.

IT MAY EXIST, BUT IT'S NOT POPULAR

Once again, Americans have made a distinction between what they feel must be allowed and what they feel comfortable with. In spite of the growing support for homosexual rights, homosexuality is still difficult for most Americans to accept as a sexual orientation or as a lifestyle.

Undoubtedly, there are few, if any, issues on which Americans' concern that fair play be demonstrated is more evident. Convinced that homosexual behavior is a personal right, most heterosexuals uphold the right of adults to engage in homosexual relationships as a matter of freedom and personal privacy. For instance, 72 percent of all adults agree that "nobody has the right to tell someone else what kind of sexual relationships they can have; it's nobody's business." The individuals who support homosexual rights most vigorously are adults who have had the highest levels of education, who live in the Northeast and in the Pacific coastal states, and who are not religious or do not view religion as very important in their lives.[3]

Millie Jackson, a black homemaker in her early sixties, is perhaps representative of the prevailing public view. "I think it's just horrible, really. But I know we must allow these things to happen or else we will become a police state and begin to lose all of our freedoms that are not what the majority want." Even many ministers appear to side with those who believe that gay rights are a necessary evil. "As a society, we must allow people to make their own choices. As a representative of God, my job is to enlighten people as to the choices God would have them make." Other ministers wholeheartedly support homosexual lifestyles. "How WASP-ish to presume that we can dictate the sexual preferences and behavior of people who differ from us," said one Episcopal minister whose congregation includes several dozen avowed homosexuals. Straying from the orthodox view of the Bible and Christian teaching, he concludes that "the Bible is a book that tells us we must accept how God leads each of us, and that exhorts all people to be loving and accepting of those who follow a different path to His love. Sexuality, in all of its forms, is a beautiful thing."

About half of all adults contend that "people who have a problem with gay lifestyles are closed-minded people." Interestingly, a number of the people who disagree with that notion support laws protecting gay lifestyles. "Sure, I have a problem with it," explained a man in his thirties from the Northeast, "but that doesn't mean I think we can outlaw it. If I'm 'closed-minded' just because I find that lifestyle distasteful or repugnant—and I do—even though I stand up for their right to live that way, then I'm not really sure what 'closed-minded' means. I guess I'd also question who is really the closed-minded party in this case, me or them."[4]

It appears that the public's willingness to acknowledge specific homosexual rights is growing, too. Gallup surveys have shown that since 1977 the public has grown increasingly tolerant of gay rights. For instance, the proportion of adults who favor extending equal rights to gays in employment opportunities has jumped from 56 percent in 1977 to 71 percent in 1989. When asked if homosexuals should be hired in each of a variety of service occupations, such as doctors, clergy, elementary school teachers, and salespersons, the proportion who accept the idea increased by anywhere between 8 and 15 percentage points during the twelve year span between 1977 and 1989.[5]

Although most people accept the idea that adults should be allowed to choose homosexual lifestyles, the public at large has not yet accepted gay couples as legitimate families. The following statistics support this contention:

- Only 22 percent of the population define two adults, living together and having a sexual relationship, as a family.
- Just one out of five adults says there is "nothing wrong with two adults of the same sex getting married to each other."
- One out of every three adults says that "gay adults should have the right to be married to each other, just as other adults are able to do."
- A mere 29 percent of the population believes that a gay couple "should be allowed to adopt children as their own family."[6]

Notice that the last two proportions are slightly higher than the first two. It is likely that this is because the last two statements concern people's beliefs about what ought to be legally permissible, while the first two reflect peoples' personal feelings about the practice of homosexual lifestyles.

Although they concede that homosexuals should have rights, and that those rights should be protected, most Americans find homosexual behavior abhorrent. For most people, it is more than just the personal repulsion they feel when they think about homosexual activity; it is a conviction that the behavior can only lead to problems, heartaches, and broken households.

Sixty-two percent of adults have stated that it is "immoral for a person to have a sexual relationship with someone of the same sex."[7] Most of those adults assert that an individual should have the right to engage in homosexual activity; yet they also believe that such behavior, while legal, is immoral.

People today are less reluctant to befriend homosexuals, but considerable resistance remains. Nationwide surveys by the *Los Angeles Times* indicate that in the mid-eighties half of the population felt uncomfortable around homosexuals. A Roper Poll in 1987 discovered that more than half of the working population said they would either strongly object to, or prefer not to work with, homosexuals.[8]

MY MOTHER IS A MAN

Most Americans reject the notion that homosexual adults can be good parents. Nine out of ten adults estimate that a child is likely to have a successful upbringing if he or she is raised by the natural parents who are happily married and living together with the child. In contrast, only 15 percent of adults believe a child is likely to have a successful upbringing if he or she were to be given up by the natural parents soon after birth and adopted by a happily married homosexual couple. (Support for the gay household came primarily from adults in the Pacific and northeastern states, and among those individuals who say that religion is not an important part of their lives.)[9]

"Oh, every time I read about these children raised by two gay women or two gay men, my heart just goes out to the children," sobbed Emily Wilkinson, a mother of three in her mid-fifties. Living in a rural community in Nebraska, she claims she has never met an adult whom she knew was homosexual. "I just don't know what I'd do, or how I'd react. Probably stare at them and wonder why." But it is not just traditional, rural housewives who shudder at the thought of homosexuality. "One of the more despicable elements of city life these days is all the weird lifestyles you're exposed to," were the words of a young man born in suburban New Jersey and who now lives in New York City. "This, in particular, is the capital of decadence. But I still get sick when I see two guys kissing, or women having a sexual encounter on the subway. Rights or no rights, it's gross. I'm not a religious fanatic, but I have to agree that there is something fundamentally wrong about that behavior. I can't see God approving it."

Not surprisingly, those most supportive of homosexual rights and practices reside within the areas of the nation that are more accepting of nontraditional lifestyles and values—the Northeast and the West Coast. Adults who are strongly in favor of permitting homosexuals to have a full scope of rights and privileges are those who have little or no interest or involvement in religious movements, churches, or philosophies. Concurrently, the people who are most adamantly opposed to homosexual behavior and values are those who express the deepest interest and involvement in their religious faith.

THE TEN PERCENT MYTH

One of the prevalent beliefs about the homosexual community—a belief that has been forcefully pushed by the gay community itself—is that homosexuals constitute about 10 percent of the population. This figure was initially suggested by eminent sex researcher Alfred Kinsey in his book *Sexual Behavior in the Human Male,* written in 1948. Kinsey reported that 10 percent of his research subjects were homosexuals, a figure that stunned the nation because it was so much higher than anticipated. Based on his research, many school systems, health care facilities, legislatures, and other institutions revised substantially the way they thought about and interacted with homosexuals.

Unfortunately, Kinsey's research methods were not adequately scrutinized until recently. The recent explorations of Kinsey's "scientific" methods have shown that his sample of subjects was so seriously flawed that his conclusions cannot in any way be applied to the population at large. For instance, his male sample included a huge proportion of prison inmates—a population known to be more prone to homosexual encounters and sexually deviant behavior. Kinsey's heavy reliance on volunteers for the interviews also undermines the reliability of the sample. In fact, the demographic character of the sample was not at all reflective of the population at large; nearly one-quarter of his sample were men previously convicted of sex offenses. Some of Kinsey's research assistants who were involved in the project have since testified that the manner in which respondents were treated in the course of the interviews probably introduced extreme bias into the data collection process.[10]

Kinsey's conclusion that 10 percent of the male population was "more or less exclusively homosexual" was accepted by the media and the homosexual community and has been treated as truth ever since. This is so even though his findings are now more than forty years old and were collected long before the sexual awakening of the late sixties. It is curious that pro-homosexual groups continue to put such faith in his work.

Even in Kinsey's report, however, it is not exactly clear how he used his own data to arrive at the 10 percent figure. He appears to have surveyed actual homosexual *contact* as well as attitudes and inclinations toward such behavior. For the latter category, he devised a rather ill-defined scale that supposedly allowed him to identify homosexuals. It seems that Kinsey, who admitted that he was seeking to persuade America to loosen up sexually, combined the statistics for all adults who embraced homosexuality either in behavior or in thought. This enabled him to arrive at the largest possible proportion—the infamous 10 percent.

Some representatives of the homosexual community have since indicated that even they do not believe that one out of every ten adults is homosexual. However, given their goal of persuading legislatures and the general public to grant rights and opportunities not currently available to them, they are happy to use the 10 percent figure, since it has widespread acceptance (especially within the mass media, among political liberals, and with those who champion the "politically correct" movement).

The gay community is not typical of groups suffering from discrimination. Usually, such groups include a large minority of the population, but are led by individuals who are poor, powerless, or both—people who seek justice against the odds. Such groups have no alternative but to fight for a bigger piece of the pie. Gaining acceptance by the masses is their only hope of fitting into the mainstream of society.

Gays lack the numbers of most popular movements but have both money and political influence. When they sense that their rights are being violated, they directly assault the prevailing powers-that-be. A Simmons Market Research Bureau study of the gay community in 1988 showed that the per capita income of homosexuals is about three times that of the general population; that they are more than three times more likely than the typical adult to have a college degree; and that they are about three times more likely than other adults to hold a professional or managerial position.[11]

Most evidence indicates that somewhere between 1 and 3 percent of the adult population engages in homosexual contact with some level of frequency.

That is hardly the profile of a down-and-out people group that is pleading for justice and mercy from a society that has forgotten them. Instead, it is the profile of a well-heeled, sophisticated group that seeks to correct a glitch in the system and is savvy enough to play within the boundaries of the system to create change.

If the Kinsey data are wrong, then what is a more accurate projection of the size of the homosexual population in America? Naturally, calculating such a number is very difficult, especially since homosexual practice remains illegal in many states. However, most evidence indicates that somewhere between 1 and 3 percent of the adult population engages in homosexual contact with some level of frequency, and that less than 1 percent might be deemed exclusively homosexual.[12] Studies conducted to date also suggest that men are about twice as likely as women to engage in homosexual behavior. Thus, somewhat less than 2 percent of the adult female population is likely to be involved in lesbian relationships.

HOW CHRISTIANS CAN RESPOND

There is little reason to expect our nation's increasing tolerance of homosexuality will be reversed anytime soon. In a nation where one of the most popular slogans among the politically active is "you can't legislate morality," and given the resurgence of liberal programs, the mid-nineties may be the time when the rights of homosexuals receive broad legal support.

It would not be surprising, for instance, to see coalitions of liberal and homosexual legislators promoting bills that broaden the rights of gays and lesbians. If they do, the nineties will be a time when more homosexuals teach in the public schools, when homosexuality will be promoted in sex education classes as a lifestyle alternative, and when millions of dollars will be committed to medical research on diseases transmitted largely within the gay population.

How should Christians react to this disturbing trend? First, we should understand God's view of homosexuality and embrace it without faltering. As Jesus demonstrated, our best response is to reject the sin while accepting the sinner. In the case of homosexual behavior, we have a significant opportunity to offer a compassionate concern for the individual, without consenting to the immoral behavior in which the person is engaged.

As we teach our youth about sexuality, Christian parents and leaders within the church must take an uncompromised, unequivocal stand against homosexual lifestyles. Rather than simply preach against it, we must become skilled at intelligently explaining God's displeasure with such aberrant behavior. The research that has "proven" a genetic cause of homosexuality is eminently flawed and must be rejected as such. When God commanded men to be with women, and not each other, He meant it.

Notes

1. The clearest biblical prohibitions on homosexuality are found in Leviticus 18:22 ("You shall not lie with a male as with a woman. It is an abomination"); Leviticus 20:13 ("If a man lies with a male like he lies with a woman, both of them have committed an abomination"); and Romans 1:27 ("Likewise also the men, leaving the natural use of the woman, burned in their lust for one another, men with men, committing what is shameful, and receiving in themselves the penalty of their error which was due").

2. George Rekers, *Growing Up Straight* (Chicago: Moody, 1982), chapters 1 and 2.

3. Data from "Family in America" survey, conducted by Barna Research Group, Ltd., in February 1992. The national random sample size was 1,009 adults.

4. Ibid.

5. This Gallup study was cited in John C. Gonsiorek and James D. Weinrich, *Homosexuality: Research Implications for Public Policy* (Newbury Park, Calif.: Sage, 1991), 61.

6. "Family in America" survey, Barna Research Group.

7. Ibid.

8. Cited in Gonsiorek and Weinrich, *Homosexuality*, 61.

9. "Family in America" survey, Barna Research Group.

10. These details can be found in Judith Reisman and Edward Eichel, *Kinsey, Sex and Fraud: The Indoctrination of a People* (Lafayette, La.: Huntington House, 1990).

11. Cited in *Sexual Disorientation*, a publication of the Family Research Council, 700 Thirteenth Street NW, Suite 500, Washington, D.C., 5.

12. There is a wide variety of evidence that confirms the 1 to 3 percent figures. Our own study, "Family in America," indicated that only 3 percent of all adults claim to have ever had sex with an individual of the same gender; 1 percent claim they will definitely or probably do so in the future. Other studies that generated similar data include two surveys from the National Opinion Research Center, one conducted in 1989, reported by Tom Smith, and the other funded by the National Science Foundation in 1991. A massive study of Minnesota adolescents, reported in the medical journal *Pediatrics*, arrived at the same outcome, as did an ongoing study of homosexual behavior conducted jointly by the Centers for Disease Control and the National Center for Health Statistics.

CHAPTER EIGHT

MINORITY FAMILIES

America has long been a country that welcomes literally millions of people from other countries. These newcomers represent a rainbow of races and ethnic backgrounds. There are, of course, some restrictions and qualifications regarding who may legally enter and remain within the country. Nevertheless, as we prepare to enter the twenty-first century, the United States has become a veritable nation of nations. The customs and values that today's immigrants have brought with them have remained in their minds, hearts, and daily routines.

Through its history, American society has expected all citizens to absorb the dominant values. Immigrants were welcome to bring their foods, styles of dress, and leisure activities, but they were also expected to learn the language and demonstrate a respect for the law, financial self-sufficiency, and esteem for traditional family forms. But over the last three decades, the consensus about family values has disappeared. With the nation's dominant social groups challenging or ignoring the historic notions of family, the distinctive lifestyles of minorities are no longer scrutinized so carefully. Many minority communities are finding a wider acceptance of their traditions in this new atmosphere of cultural pluralism.

To understand fully the changes besetting the traditional notion of family and to gain a glimpse into what the family of the future might look like, it is critical to observe family systems in some of America's minority communities. In this chapter, we will investigate the family in the black and Hispanic communities, the two dominant minority cultures in America today.[1]

THE AMERICAN GROWTH EXPERIENCE

Population growth is a dominant theme of American history. During this century, the population of the United States has more than tripled, growing by 230 percent! The population grew by at least 10 percent in every decade between 1900 and 1979. During the latter half of the century, however, the rate of expansion steadily declined. In the fifties, the population grew by nearly 19 percent. In the sixties, the rate slipped to about 13 percent, then to 11 percent in the seventies. The eighties registered slightly less than a 10 percent expansion. The nineties are expected to witness a continued slowing of the rate of growth, dipping into the single digits, probably to around 7 or 8 percent.[2]

What is most interesting about the aggregate population increase is that the growth can no longer be attributed almost exclusively to native-born white women having children. These days, immigration plays a major and increasing role in our population expansion—both in terms of the number of immigrants arriving and in the numbers of children that immigrant women bear each year.

Immigration is on the upswing in America, and the limitations on those who wish to enter the country have eased considerably. Beginning in 1924, most foreigners who had sought legal residence in America were turned back, dramatically reversing the decades-long policy of easy entrance to immigrants who wanted to settle in the country. During the first quarter of this century, some 15 million immigrants were granted legal residence or citizenship here. From the late twenties and through the late forties, however, barely 2 million additional immigrants were accepted.[3]

After the end of World War II and the return to business-as-usual, the need for more low-wage laborers, combined with the end of wartime tensions and the reduced fear of enemy infiltrators, spurred a revival in immigration. In the 1950s, more than 2.5 million newcomers became American citizens. That figure continued to grow each decade: 3.3 million legal immigrants in the sixties, 4.5 million in the seventies, 5.8 million in the eighties. In the nineties, barring unforeseen political shifts, we will likely eclipse the seven million mark for the first time in nearly ninety years.[4]

As the statistics in Table 8.1 show, immigration is an increasingly important element in our overall population growth. Because America's rate of growth is declining, the continual increase in the number of immigrants entering the nation means that a higher proportion of the overall growth can be attributed directly to immigration. So, although immigration was responsible for just 9 percent of the growth in the fifties, it will likely account for nearly 40 percent of the expansion we realize in the nineties.

At the turn of the century, more than 80 percent of all immigrants came to the U.S. from European nations. Today, the pattern is remarkably different. Less than 10 percent of our immigrants come from European countries. America is gaining its immigrants from two areas of the world: Latino or Hispanic nations (Central America, Mexico, and South America) and southeastern Asian nations. Together, Hispanic and Asian immigrants make up about two-thirds of America's new residents each year.[5]

HISPANIC FAMILIES

Hispanic adults who come to America tend to preserve the family traditions that make up their heritage. They also tend to have larger families than most Americans. There are several reasons for this:

- Hispanic adults who come to America are predominantly Catholic. The Catholic church, especially in the less industrialized nations in which it is strong, has continued to promote the view that large families are a sign of God's blessing.

■ Hispanic immigrants come from cultures that attach a greater significance to the family, which governs the behavior of its members and is a source of stability and pride.

■ For men in many Hispanic or Latin cultures, living up to the role of the "macho man" is still common; one of the external signs of such *machismo* is fathering numerous children.

■ Many Hispanics who settle in America come from agricultural nations that regard children as important laborers in the fields, in the marketplace, and in home child care.

■ Most Hispanics come from nations that are neither familiar nor comfortable with recent innovations in birth control. (And, being strict Catholics, many of them accept their church's teaching against the use of birth control devices or pills.)

■ Similarly, Hispanics are less likely to accept abortion as an acceptable means of ending an unwanted pregnancy.

The average household size among whites in America is 2.5 people; among Hispanics, it is 3.4. (See Table 8.2 for some demographic differences between white, Hispanic, and black families.) This is a reflection of the greater esteem Hispanics place on both marriage and childbearing. To most Hispanic women, being a homemaker is an ideal, not the "cultural slavery" that many American feminists consider it to be.

This larger family size is especially meaningful when you take into account the harsh socioeconomic realities facing Hispanics in America. They have an above-average unemployment rate; a below-average literacy rate; a substantially below-average household income level (in 1989, the median was $21,921, which was 28 percent below the white median); and live in smaller quarters. In fact, about one-quarter of all Hispanic families and 36 percent of all Hispanic children in America live below the poverty level.[6]

The willingness to have larger families in spite of such conditions is powerful testimony to the critical difference between the dominant American view of family and the prevailing Hispanic view. Presently, most native-born adults think of having children in practical

TABLE 8.1 Population Growth Due to Immigration

Decade	Increase in population	Number of immigrants	Percentage of population growth due to immigration
1900–1909	16.3 MILLION	8.8 MILLION	53.9 %
1910–1919	14.1 MILLION	5.7 MILLION	40.8%
1920–1929	16.6 MILLION	4.1 MILLION	24.7%
1930–1939	9.4 MILLION	0.5 MILLION	5.6%
1940–1949	19.8 MILLION	1.0 MILLION	5.2%
1950–1959	28.4 MILLION	2.5 MILLION	8.8%
1960–1969	23.3 MILLION	3.3 MILLION	14.2%
1970–1979	22.7 MILLION	4.2 MILLION	18.7%
1980–1989	22.3 MILLION	6.3 MILLION	28.5%
1990–1999	18.7 MILLION	7.2 MILLION	38.7%

Source: *Statistical Abstract of the United States, 1991,* and *Historical Statistics: Colonial Times to 1970,* U.S. Bureau of the Census, Series P-25. The data for the 1990–1999 decade are projections based upon current population trends and estimates of future behavior.

terms: it is something to be pursued when the economic and social conditions are right for such a commitment. Hispanics tend to reflect different priorities. They are more likely to perceive family to be a core element in life, one which is best pursued at the earliest possible time. Finances, housing, relationships, and all other lifestyle factors all follow from the needs of the family.

Given the higher priority Hispanics place upon marriage and family, it is not surprising to learn that the divorce rate among Hispanics is lower than among the white population. However, the lure of easy divorce is beginning to erode the commitment that Hispanics tradition-ally bring to marriage, despite the fact that divorce runs counter to the teachings of the Catholic church. Whereas there were substantial differ-ences between the white and Hispanic divorce rates twenty years ago, today the gap is closing. Currently, 21 percent of the adult white population has been divorced at some time; among Hispanics, the figure has risen to 17 percent.[7] Overall, one-third of all Hispanic families are headed by a single parent; in more than nine out of ten cases, the mother retains custody of the children.[8]

There is mounting evidence that Hispanics are experiencing a breakdown in their traditional family values much the way other family systems in America have. For instance, the proportion of Hispanic women getting abortions is apparently on the rise. Cohabitation is also increasingly frequent among Hispanic adults, even outpacing the na-tional figures in some cases. Hispanic women are twice as likely as white women to be unwed mothers; one-third of all live births to Hispanic women in 1988 were to single women.[9]

HISPANICS THINK DIFFERENTLY ABOUT FAMILY

Hispanics maintain many of their traditional views about family. Seven out of ten concur that if the traditional family unit falls apart, American society itself will collapse. Nine out of ten agree that it is more difficult to raise a child successfully as a single parent than as part of a married couple. Eight out of ten believe that God intended marriage to last a lifetime. Two out of three Hispanic adults also feel that legal marriages should be encouraged, since this kind of commitment brings about a stability that cohabitation or other alternative families cannot provide.[10]

But the abandonment of traditional views of family and the increasing doubt about the viability of marriage is evident in other attitudes expressed by Hispanics. For instance, two-thirds of the Hispanic adults interviewed provided a nouveau definition of family. (See chapter 2 for more on nouveau families.) Although Hispanic adults are quick to acknowledge the danger in divorce, they are also becoming more accepting of it. Six out of ten Hispanics believe that being raised in a single-parent household puts the child at a disadvantage. Just one out of three Hispanics believes that a child is likely to have a very successful upbringing if his or her parents are divorced and the child is raised by a single-parent mother. Yet a whopping 72 percent of the Hispanic population in this country claims that most people who get married these days will wind up divorced within five years! (That proportion is about 45 percent higher than the national average.) Most Hispanics agree that marriage will soon be replaced by cohabitation, making them the only ethnic group in which more than half of the respondents anticipated this outcome. And half of the Hispanic people interviewed said that anyone who gets married these days is fighting the odds, because it is "almost impossible to have a successful marriage these days." In fact, a slim majority now say that it is best to live with a future spouse for a while before the marriage. Again, Hispanics are now the only ethnic group among whom a majority condone such behavior.[11] (See Table 8.2 for a detailed look at white, Hispanic, and black attitudes toward family life.)

Overall, Hispanics, more than any other ethnic group studied, feel a sense of loss over the deterioration of their traditional family structure. They are the least likely to expect America to return to the traditional family values of the fifties (only 22 percent anticipate such a turn of events). And they are more than twice as likely as white adults to describe marriage as an "outdated idea . . . that does not fit American culture these days." Although they are as likely as any other segment to believe that marriage should be conceived as a permanent arrangement between two people, they are also twice as likely as other adults to say that a person is better off these days remaining single and unmarried than getting married.[12]

The nineties, then, represent a turning point for Hispanics. It is the decade in which they will probably reject the values they brought with them and reluctantly embrace the superficial American replacements. Even now, partly in response to new economic opportunities, many are adopting the American ideal: identifying career and lifestyle goals, setting priorities according to those goals, and then building a family around those higher priorities. This approach is especially noticeable among second- and third-generation Hispanic-Americans. The further the immigrant families get from the "old country" ideals and values, the more likely they are to embrace the prevailing perspectives of the culture in which they live.[13]

BLACK AMERICAN FAMILIES

Understanding the African American family requires an entirely different perspective. Whereas a large percentage of the Hispanics in the United States are first- or second-generation Americans, most blacks living in this country have a heritage that goes back several generations. Blacks do not struggle with the pressures of assimilation into a new culture; theirs is the war to survive urban poverty and economic inequality. Their religious legacy, like that of most Hispanic immigrants, is strong and significant, but it is predominantly Protestant rather than Catholic. Blacks have also endured decades of racial prejudice that in some respects remains as strong as ever.

The character of the black family has been shaped by its historical experience. This helps explain why the black family differs markedly from other ethnic or racial groups. Statistics demonstrate the plight of this group. From cradle to grave, it is not a pretty picture.

■ A majority of black adults are not married. Sixty-one percent of both the white and Hispanic adult populations are currently married, but just 44 percent of all black adults fit this category.[14]

TABLE
8.2
Race/Ethnicity and the American Family

How Families Differ by Race/Ethnicity

Characteristic/demographic	Caucasians	Hispanics	Blacks
Number of people in household	2.5	3.4	2.8
Median household income	$30,406	$21,921	$18,083
Children living with both parents	81%	69%	41%
Families below the poverty line	8%	23%	28%
Live births to unwed mothers	18%	64%	34%

Source: *Statistical Abstract of the United States, 1991*, U.S. Dept. of Commerce, Bureau of the Census.

How Attitudes Differ by Race/Ethnicity

Statement about family life	Percent who agree		
	Caucasians	Hispanics	Blacks
People getting married these days are fighting the odds; it's almost impossible to have a successful marriage these days.	31%	50%	27%
Before getting married, it's best to live with that person for a while.	37%	51%	44%
Within the next few years, most people who get married will get divorced within their first five years.	50%	72%	47%
Within the next few years, marriage will be replaced by living together.	35%	55%	45%
Being raised in a single-parent home puts a child at a disadvantage in life.	60%	58%	48%
It's not as much fun raising a child as it used to be.	38%	39%	57%
It's better to go through life being single and unmarried than to get married.	14%	29%	18%

Source: "Family in America" survey conducted in February 1992 by the Barna Research Group, Ltd. These data reflect the views of the 1,009 people interviewed in the study. The percentages exceed 100 percent because each person was allowed to give multiple answers.

- The divorce rate among blacks is the highest of any racial or ethnic group in America, presently in excess of 60 percent.
- Sixty-four percent of black children under the age of eighteen live in homes in which one or both parents are absent.[15] More than three-quarters of all black children born this year will live in a single-parent or no-parent home before reaching the age of eighteen.
- Almost two out of three black women who give birth to children are not married at the time of the birth. The proportion of black teenage girls giving birth to children is twice that of white teenage girls.[16]
- The abortion rate among black women is more than double that of white women.[17]
- Economically, millions of black families are in dire straits: three out of ten black families live below the poverty line; nearly 43 percent of all black children under eighteen do.[18] In fact, the median household income of whites is about 70 percent higher than that of blacks; even Hispanics have a median household income that is more than 20 percent above that of blacks.[19]

These statistics, and others in the same vein, tell us little about the human turmoil behind the numbers. However, they do point out many of the reasons for the shattered hope, despair, and turbulence that many blacks feel.

It seems irrefutably clear that many black adults accept the notion that the traditional family structure, while desirable, is not necessary for creating a successful family. Whites and Hispanics tend to regard divorce as a life-shattering experience; to blacks, it is undesirable and unfortunate, but generally not paralyzing. A majority of black adults contend that a successful marriage is possible these days, yet half of them expect most new marriages to end in divorce within five years. Most believe that marriage is still a relevant concept for our society; that getting legally married is important to providing a stable family; and that God intended marriage to be once and for all.

Despite the high incidence of failed marriages and broken families, many blacks maintain a sense of optimism and perseverance. In other words, the marriage may fail, but the individuals will prevail. Black adults are less likely than any others to fear that our society will crumble if the traditional family unit falls apart. They have a strong sense that community is important and that a strong society requires networks of supportive relationships, but they do not believe that the key relationships involve only the nuclear family. They are just as likely to perceive an extended family as being the core of a strong society.[20]

Most blacks admit that raising children is not as much fun these days as it used to be.[21] Blacks are also less likely than other racial or ethnic groups to contend that being a single-parent is tougher than being part of a married couple who raises children. Similarly, they are less likely to suggest that a child in a single-parent home is at a developmental disadvantage. And they are more likely than other adults to believe that a single mother raising her children can do so successfully, without a husband present.[22]

In the coming decade, the attitudes and values of black and Hispanic families will greatly influence the character of American families.

In many black communities we see the strong imprint of nouveau family ideas. In fact, the very model of the nouveau family has much in common with the black family experience. It seems reasonable to suggest that although blacks do not champion the end of the traditional family, they have become relatively comfortable with alternative family forms. There are several reasons for this. First, they have persevered at cultivating a keen sense of extended community, which compensates for the weakened nuclear family. Second, divorce has come to be regarded as an unfortunate but widely shared experience. And third, black women have become comfortable with the notion that they will ultimately be responsible for their own economic and emotional survival and, in all probability, that of the children they bear.

HOW CHRISTIANS CAN RESPOND

In the coming decade, the attitudes and values of black and Hispanic families will greatly influence the character of American families. Americans should not underestimate their potential cultural impact. During the latter half of the nineties, the white population will be producing children at a zero population growth rate—in other words, this group is not producing enough children to maintain its numbers in the overall population. At the same time the black, Hispanic, and Asian populations will grow at a pace well beyond the rate of replacement. Thus, minority groups will have a more visible presence in the ongoing debate over family values.

Given their pride in their heritage and their attachment to community, minority families stand a better chance of retaining many of the values and strengths inherent in traditional family systems. What can the church do to enhance that potential? First, we can encourage ethnic families to maintain their extended family ties. Many ethnic clans have not yet allowed the lure of material prosperity and upward mobility to tear apart their cohesiveness. The value of having an extended family system has been well-documented—and virtually lost to most Americans. Broader family relationships often prove to be helpful in transmitting important values, in supporting the efforts of young families, and in passing on a sense of heritage, and the church should nurture these family ties.

Ethnic families would also benefit by conveying their cultural heritage to their children. The values that Hispanics, blacks, Asians and others bring to America from their homelands not only make them unique but also shelter them from the often-bankrupt ideas pushed at them by contemporary American society. We should applaud the traditions within immigrant cultures that share similarities with biblical concepts. Rather than urging these people to become more like white, middle-class Americans, the church would be wise to appreciate and celebrate the uniqueness of immigrants. By providing them with social acceptance without pressuring them to adopt the "American way," the Christian church in this nation could enhance the self-esteem, assimilation, and spiritual development of these people.

Beyond that, Christians should help ethnic believers to develop strong churches. Such communities of faith could encourage newcomers to identify with their heritage and provide the support they need to live effectively within American society. Instead of attempting to plant (or expand) churches that assimilate immigrants into the white churches, immigrants and ethnic groups should have the option of joining a community of believers who share a similar culture and values.

Notes

1. Ideally, this chapter would include a discussion of Asian immigrant families. Unfortunately, not enough credible research has been done to support a meaningful analysis of these groups.

2. *Statistical Abstract of the United States, 1991*, U.S. Dept. of Commerce, Bureau of the Census, Washington, D.C., 1991; tables 1-2, p. 7.

3. Ibid., table 5, p. 9.

4. Ibid.

5. Ibid., table 7, p. 10.

6. Ibid., table 60, p. 47; table 225, p. 139; table 227, p. 140; table 255, p. 155; table 722, p. 449; table 746, p. 462; and table 751, p. 464.

7. These data are based on a variety of national telephone and mail surveys conducted by the Barna Research Group.

8. *Statistical Abstract of the United States, 1991*, table 69, p. 52.

9. Data in this section come from Barna Research studies conducted over the past decade; data provided by the Alan Guttmacher Institute, New York; and from *Statistical Abstract of the United States, 1991*, table 89, p. 66.

10. Data from "Family in America" survey, conducted by Barna Research Group, Ltd., in February 1992. The national random sample size was 1,009 adults.

11. Ibid.

12. Ibid.

13. Such conclusions have been drawn by various analysts based on a number of studies. See Yankelovich, Skelley & White, "Hispanic USA" (New York, 1984); Frank L. Schick and Rene Schick, eds., *Statistical Handbook on U.S. Hispanics* (Phoenix: Oryx, 1986); and studies conducted by Barna Research since 1984.

14. See "Marital Status and Living Arrangements: March 1991," U.S. Dept. of Commerce, Bureau of the Census, series P-20, #461, April 1992.

15. Ibid.

16. *Statistical Abstract of the United States, 1991*, table 89, p. 66.

17. Ibid., table 102, p. 71.

18. Ibid., table 746, p. 462, and table 751, p. 464.

19. Ibid., table 722, p. 449.

20. "Family in America" survey, Barna Research Group.
21. Ibid.
22. Ibid.

CHAPTER NINE

MAKING TIME
FOR FAMILY

More than any other resource, time has become the currency of the nineties. If you want to understand how highly people value something, look at how much time they give to it.

With the crush of duties and opportunities pressing down on contemporary adults, family is but one element clamoring for time—always more and more time, it seems. How satisfactorily have adults arranged their schedules to reflect their commitment to family needs and interests? By their own admission, not too well. Consider these recent research findings:

- According to a nationwide survey conducted by the *Los Angeles Times* in 1990, most parents (56 percent) feel guilty about not spending enough time with their children.
- Working adults feel tension between their commitments to job and family. A study undertaken by the *New York Times* in 1989 noted that among employed adults with children

in their household, three out of four said that they are torn between committing themselves to their jobs and concentrating on the needs of their families.

■ A study in 1991 by the National Commission on Children reported that six out of ten parents want to spend more time with their families.

■ A nationwide survey conducted for *USA Today* revealed that among households with two parents present, 73 percent would have one of the parents stay at home with the children if money were not an issue.

■ A survey by Yankelovich Clancy Schulman revealed that the proportion of working women who would like to quit working if they could get by without the money they earn has been increasing for the last several years; currently, about six out of ten employed females express such a desire.[1]

Our research indicates that millions of American adults feel trapped by demands that do not reflect their personal priorities and preferences in life. Although they might like to allocate a greater portion of their waking hours to family or other leisure activities, their financial obligations or other needs preclude it. "Sometimes, having a family feels like a noose around my neck," explained a woman in her mid-forties who has three primary school children. She works thirty hours a week at a nearby small business to help her family get by financially. "I'd much rather spend my time with my kids or my husband, but we just can't afford it right now. It makes me feel bad because I blame the family for putting such pressure on me. But it's not really family, it's other circumstances that are really putting on the pressure."

In a society in which nearly one-third of all adults claim to be "stressed out," and less than one-quarter of all adults contend that they make enough money to live comfortably, one of the major challenges of coping with life successfully is determining how to divvy up one's limited time. The importance a person attaches to family will usually determine how he or she spends a typical day.[2]

MAKING TIME COUNT

Americans are generally achievement-driven. At school, grades tell us how adequately a student has completed the assigned tasks. On the job, our supervisors spell out goals and measure our performance against those expectations. Even in leisure endeavors, Americans are increasingly performance-driven, setting goals for exercise, for logging frequent flyer miles, for reading a certain number of books, and so on. Those who view their free time as a period for "vegging out" without achieving anything are frequently lampooned as sluggards who will never fulfill their dreams. Even people who complain about the conflict between achieving personal goals and meeting family demands find few sympathetic ears these days. Caring for a spouse and offspring or tending to household duties is generally dismissed as a lame excuse for diminished productivity.

Even families feel the need to parcel out time for themselves. Millions of adults now hold weekly planning sessions to determine how they will spend their limited hours together. Adults living in a family household have 168 hours available and spend an average of about 56 of those hours sleeping. That leaves 112 hours to make the most of. For the typical adult in a married couple household, employment duties capture the lion's share of the weekday hours. Among men, roughly 50 of the 112 non-sleep hours are consumed by work-related activities: doing their job, commuting to and from the job, and taking an hour each day for lunch. (Women typically devote fewer hours to their paying job, the difference being made up by the non-paying, household jobs they do.)

During the last decade, the meaning of "work" has changed appreciably. Work used to provide us with a sense of self-worth and sharpened our identity. Today, however, Americans tend to see work as a means to an end: namely, as a way of providing enough cash to live the kind of life they can truly enjoy. Thus, it was surprising to discover a Gallup Poll in 1990 that showed 54 percent of Americans in favor of moving from a five-day work week to a four-day work schedule with longer daily shifts. Just one decade earlier, fewer than four out of ten adults had advocated such a change.[3]

What is behind the enthusiasm for the four-day work week? With increased time pressure, greater numbers of dual-income families, and a faster pace of life putting new stresses and strains on families, fewer people are pursuing occupational achievement to the exclusion of all else. The majority of individuals opting for the transition to a four-day work calendar were motivated by the desire to have longer unbroken blocks of time for their leisure pursuits. It is significant to note that the hope of spending more time with family was one of the compelling advantages of the four-day week.[4]

Some adults want to work fewer days because they have a plan for how they'd use the extra days off. "It's tough enough having to work for a living just to get by," was the retort of Andie Speroza, a working mother in her mid-thirties. "I would think that employers would be more understanding of the difficulties we [working mothers] face and help out when they can. Permitting a four-day work week would certainly help." Others can identify with Tom Ellingsworth, an executive for a national chain of shoe stores, who remarked, "We've discussed the option at our regional planning meetings, and it may yet come to pass. It would certainly alter my lifestyle. I can't imagine what I'd do with an extra day off each week; what a dream that would be. I'm sure it'd get filled up quickly, but it sure sounds like a wonderful idea."

Many adults have already rearranged their daily schedules to adjust for their changing priorities. They have committed more time to family matters, their jobs, pleasure reading, and physical workouts; and less time to friends, volunteer work, involvement in churches and religious groups, and television watching. (Take a look at the figures in Table 9.1 for the details of this time-shifting phenomenon.)

When we asked adults to estimate the number of hours they spend on various activities in a typical week, career and relational inter-action topped the list. By their own account, they spend more than twenty hours a week doing a wide range of activities with family members. In fact, 69 percent of all married people say they spend more than 10 hours a week with their spouse, and 45 percent of all parents say they devote in excess of ten hours a week to their children. The typical American adult spends three hours per week with close personal friends and about four more hours interacting with people they know from their job. The remainder of their time is consumed by personal hygiene, household chores, shopping, health care, and so on.[5]

TABLE
9.1 How Americans Are Reallocating Their Time

Compared to one year ago, are you now spending more time, less time, or about the same amount of time as a year ago on these activities?

Activity

Percentage spending

Activity	More time	About the same	Less time
At home with your family	43%	41%	14%
Working at your job	39%	39%	17%
Reading for pleasure	34%	38%	27%
Exercising, working out	34%	37%	28%
Seeking additional formal education	30%	37%	34%
With friends	26%	42%	30%
Volunteering time	22%	45%	32%
Participating in church or religious activities	20%	44%	33%
Watching television	18%	40%	42%

Source: George Barna, *What Americans Believe* (Ventura, Calif.: Regal, 1991), 49–76.

MARRIED TIME VS. SINGLE TIME

The ways married couples spend their free time differ from those of single adults in several ways. First, married adults commit fewer hours to building and maintaining nonfamily relationships. In contrast, never-married adults spend twice as many hours each week (about seven) with close friends, more than four times as many hours interacting with their parents, and an extra hour or two with people they know from their school or place of employment.[6]

Divorced adults who have children tend to allocate their time in ways very similar to that of married couples, except that they spend several fewer hours per week with their children (probably due to custody arrangements). Widowed adults actually spend more time in an average week with their children and grandchildren than divorced parents spend with their kids. Widowed adults also spend more time with neighbors than do any others: they devote nearly two hours per week to such relationships, whereas all others allocate less than one-half hour per week to time with neighbors.[7]

A second difference relates to the activities deemed most enjoyable by people in different stages of family life. Participating in sports or athletics is the favorite leisure activity of all adults (named by 23 percent), followed by reading (17 percent) and socializing (11 percent). The family focus of married adults is evident even in their leisure adventures: they are more likely than single people to engage in family activities and in hobbies, but less likely to invest themselves in nonfamily socializing and in cultural endeavors (such as art, music, and photography).[8]

Most parents do not readily acknowledge that having children dramatically alters the kinds of activities in which they participate. However, an examination of the typical activity calendar reveals vast differences between families with children and childless adults. Parents are more likely than others to use television viewing as a family experience (86 percent do so in a typical week); to take a trip to a special place specifically for the enjoyment of the children (59 percent say they do so in any given week); to spend time on educational activities for the family, such as helping children with homework or going on educational trips together (73 percent); or to talk for more than thirty minutes with a child about things of importance to that child (80 percent). (See Table 9.2 for a summary of these findings.) Parents spend time in activities similar to those of unmarried individuals, but they are less likely to go out for a fun meal, play a sport, experience some kind of cultural event, or go to a theater to see a movie.[9]

A father of five young children from the Northwest explained his view of family time. "TV gets criticized a lot as an idiot box. In our household, we have rules about who can watch what programs, and how much time the kids can spend in front of the set. Usually, we're traveling together to team sports. When we do watch TV, it's usually as a family. A lot of times the kids ask questions about what they've just watched and that gives us an easy entrée into talking about values and how people live. Sometimes we take trips to places that we see covered in the news or on local programs. TV has actually been an initiator of more family time for us." Although we found that parents were more likely to express negative views about television viewing by their kids, it was also apparent that TV time represents a significant portion of today's family life.

In general, Americans want to squeeze out more time for family. Even people who are divorced, widowed, or have children but are not married seem determined to strike a more even balance between career, family, and personal leisure pursuits. And although many parents express a desire to make family a higher priority, career demands limit how much time they have for family-related interaction.

THE RISE OF THE WORKING WOMAN

It would be a major oversight to omit a discussion of the working woman from our discussion of family time. Not only has this development affected families profoundly, it has also generated controversy over the role of women in today's society.

Some of the information related to the unprecedented expansion in the number of working women has been well-publicized and appears to be accurate. The proportion of married women who are employed and have children under the age of six has doubled, rising from 30 percent in 1970 to 58 percent in 1989. During that same time, the proportion of married women who work and have school-age children in the home has jumped from 49 percent to 73 percent. Currently, among divorced women with children under six, three-quarters are employed, and 85 percent of divorced women with school-age kids are working. Women with children are actually more likely to hold a job than are women who have no kids in the home, regardless of their marital status.[10]

The kinds of jobs held by women have changed significantly also. Whereas women used to seek jobs that would provide income with minimal stress and responsibility, today women seek—and receive—more responsible and demanding positions. Instead of filling routine roles and entry-level positions, women have entered the management ranks in considerable numbers. The Bureau of Labor Statistics reports that in the last decade the proportion of managers who are women has grown from 27 percent to 41 percent.[11] Other data show that of all new businesses formed in 1992, a majority of them will be initiated or headed by a woman.

These data help explain why the median salary earned by married females, working either full-time or part-time, has increased to $16,512.[12] Among full-time employed women, the aggregate annual income they earn is just 68 percent as much as men employed full-time—a positive leap from the 60 percent they made in 1980, but still a substantial difference.[13]

However, the Bureau of Labor Statistics also found that the proportion of senior corporate executives who are women has barely changed in the last ten years, rising from 1 percent to just 3 percent. Women are pessimistic about breaking the "glass ceiling" and emerging at the top anytime in the near future. A Business Week poll of 400 female managers noted that six out of ten believe that career growth opportunities for women have died; seven out of ten believe that corporations are male-dominated and that such authority among men will preclude further career progress for women; and less than half say that a woman in the corporate world has the same chance as a male to get promoted.[14]

The plight of Laura Wilson is typical. Married and a mother of two young children ages six and nine, she drops the kids off at a

TABLE
9.2 # How Adults Spend Their Family Time

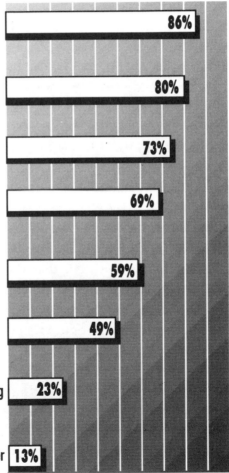

Family activity

Percentage who engaged in this
activity during the past week

Watched television together as a family **86%**

Spent more than 30 minutes at a time
talking with your child about things that
are important to the child **80%**

Spent time doing homework or other
educational activities together **73%**

Went out to a restaurant for a fun meal
together **69%**

Took a trip to a special place chosen
because the children would enjoy it **59%**

Played some type of sport together **49%**

Attended or experienced some type of
cultural activity as a family, such as going
to a museum, a play, or a concert **23%**

Went to a theater to see a movie together **13%**

Source: "Family in America" survey conducted in February 1992 by the Barna Research Group, Ltd. These data reflect the views of
the 375 parents in the study who have children under 18 living in the home.

neighbor's house at 7:30 each morning on her way to work (the neighbor takes the kids to school). Laura has arranged for her children to be dropped off at a day care center after school and picks them up on the way home at 6:00 each evening. "At first I felt guilty about neglecting the kids, but now I think we've all made the adjustment. It works out fine. I'm exhausted at the end of a day, but overall life is working."

Laura holds a middle management position and wants to jump into the company hierarchy in the next five years. The exhaustion brought on by juggling career, family, and personal life is compounded by her need to take home an hour or two of work each night. Like so many women in her position, she sees few alternatives. "If I wait until the kids are grown and out of the house to enter the job market, I'd never have a chance to impact the business world because the quality of jobs they give to a fifty-year-old entering the market are really entry-level and don't lead anywhere. Besides, working for me is a necessity. To live at the level and lifestyle we desire, we could never do it on Dan's salary alone."

UNMASKING THE HIDDEN TRUTHS

At the same time that women are making substantial gains in the business world, there are a number of facts about working women that have rarely seen the light of day. Although most women do work, a high proportion of them work part-time—especially mothers of young children. A recent analysis of employment data revealed that about six out of ten women are in the labor force but that the majority of them actually work part-time, some as little as three hours per week.[15]

Although it is true that women who work full-time earn less than men who work full-time, a significant part of the explanation relates to the different levels of experience and responsibility held by men and women. Recent research also indicates that part of the reason why women fail to reach the highest levels of authority in corporations is simply because they do not aspire to those positions.[16] "If men want to rule the corporate jungle, they can have it," was the feeling of Jana Bunnel. "I just want to make a decent living, enough to live comfortably and put my kids through school. I work out of necessity. I have no illusions of becoming Ted Turner in a skirt and blouse."

In still other ways, the plight of working women (especially single-parent working women) is probably much different than is commonly assumed. For instance, a considerable portion of the pressure to stabilize household finances falls upon the woman's shoulders. Consequently, since 1969, the number of women holding two or more jobs has quintupled.[17] And while the typical working mother has added a paying job to her list of responsibilities, most families expect her to do the same household chores she did before accepting the outside job. Working women, when their paid employment and household duties are jointly considered, work about fifteen hours per week more than their husbands. Over the course of a year, that adds up to more than one full month of twenty four-hour days of work.[18]

More and more mothers. . .are actively seeking ways of exiting the labor force so that they can devote their full attention to the needs of their families.

"I always feel tired," insisted Molly Cervantes, a twenty-eight-year-old mother of two and full-time employee of a department store. "Is that normal? I'm supposed to be 'young,' but it sure doesn't feel that way." When asked if she believes that her packed schedule—kids, work, church, friends, hobbies (she loves bowling and tennis), and community work—increases her feelings of stress, she denies the allegation. "No," she declared, "you have to take advantage of what's available out there. Nobody is going to take care of you, and no one is going to cry for you if you feel like you're not enjoying life. It is a busy life, but I'm getting to do all the things that I want and that are important to me and my family."

Most working women do not get the credit they deserve for fulfilling their demanding workloads. Nine out of ten adults believe that when both the husband and wife are working full-time, the family and household responsibilities should be equally shared. Yet, according to such couples, only about one couple out of eight divides those labors equally. When confronted with such facts, few adults express surprise—

and just as few defend the fact that the gap between what is and what they believe should be is so wide.[19]

WILTING UNDER THE PRESSURE

The "second shift" that women work at home after spending time at a job is wearing down millions of women. Reports of illnesses, acute fatigue, emotional exhaustion, depression, and unfulfilled expectations suggest that many women are not satisfied with their existence. Even the forms of assistance designed to make the "super mom" possible, such as child-care centers, have failed to provide the kind of help that women need. Thus, although American families now spend in excess of $16 billion each year on child care, increasing proportions of people say that leaving a child in a care facility day after day is likely to scar the child for life. Large percentages of people believe that a child who does not have full-time parenting grows up with a disadvantage. More and more mothers, according to recent surveys, say that they are actively seeking ways of exiting the labor force so that they can devote their full attention to the needs of their families.[20]

In 1991, a Roper Poll of women nationwide found that for the first time in ten years, women's top lifestyle preference was no longer a career along with a family. After nearly two decades of experimenting with new responsibilities and pressures, women are increasingly indicating that they have had enough of the "liberated" lifestyle and would opt for a more traditional role if possible.[21]

Adding to the curious reversal of attitudes is that American men, who initially resisted the prospect of their wives assuming the dual tasks of mother and associate breadwinner, overwhelmingly approve of women working outside the home these days. Currently, nine out of ten men under 30 believe that women should be allowed to work, regardless of their family circumstances.[22] "They want to make decisions that impact their lives. They want the right to control their bodies, like in the abortion issue. They want the right to have their own credit lines and credit cards," said Dale Rivers, a middle-aged cab driver from St. Louis, who shrugs his shoulders and accepts the new way of life. "So, sure, they want to have independence in the work place, too. It's the way things are these days. There's not much difference in the roles of men and women, other than the biological differences." Like many men, Dale seems more resigned to the fact than enthusiastic about it.

FAMILY FINANCES AND WORKING WOMEN

Naturally, given the growing disenchantment among women with employment away from home, the impetus that keeps them working must be compelling. And for most working women, it is. They typically work because they feel they have to: 57 percent say that they need the money. A small percentage of working women are driven by the desire to be productive or to make it in a man's world (27 percent), while an even smaller number works as a means of developing relationships or having contact with other people (7 percent) or simply to occupy their free time (mentioned by 5 percent, mostly older women whose children had left home).[23] A majority of working women (56 percent) insist that they would quit their job today if they did not need the money; this figure is up from 33 percent in 1988.[24]

Many working women also sense the tension of holding a job and sustaining a marriage. Research by Andrew Greeley and National Opinion Research Center found that, when lifestyle conditions are statistically accounted for, working mothers are more likely than homemakers to get divorced. (The research also found that frequent sexual intercourse and joint prayer between husband and wife can effectively eliminate that probability.)[25]

Nor is it true, as some analysts have proposed, that working women are simply "a different breed of woman," individuals who have a less powerful maternal or family instinct and are more emotionally drawn and designed to compete in the business world. Our studies show that women, whether they work outside the home or not, have essentially undifferentiated views about the realities, priorities, and satisfactions of work and family.

GROWING SUPPORT FOR WOMAN AS MOM

In the mid-seventies, most adults supported women's entry into the labor force. They believed that the family could handle the absence of a mother who performed traditional household duties. Currently, though, the pendulum has swung in the opposite direction. Studies and anecdotal evidence suggest that women who work pay a heavy price for their occupational endeavors. It is no longer simply the avowed homemakers who contend that the financial rewards reaped by women on the job pale in comparison to the rewards earned by sacrificing such employment. "If I had a chance to do my life over again," dreamed Beth Stockton, a full-time customer service representative working for a cable television company, "I'd have just stayed home with the kids. Work has allowed us to have a more comfortable life materially, but it has robbed me and my kids of a lot of important time and togetherness. I don't think it's been worth it."

In a sense, tens of millions of women have become economic slaves, working against their own will or best interests. Note, for example, that our recent survey found that most adults believe that a married couple with two children is more likely to be happy and content if the father works full-time and the mother stays home with the children than if both parents work full-time. In fact, Americans favor this more traditional model by a four to one margin (72 percent versus 17 percent)—a ratio that represents equally the view of married adults, singles, divorced people, parents, and both working and nonworking women![26]

HOW CHRISTIANS CAN RESPOND

Don't be surprised if you see more and more technology being used to solve some of the conflicts working women face. By using modems, telephones, fax machines, personal computers, picture phones, compact discs, and other recent innovations, millions of women are likely to assume service-based jobs that they can do from their homes, on a flexible schedule, enabling them to juggle family and career duties more easily. These technological advances don't discriminate, though. More and more men will likely work from the home on a part-time basis, further improving their involvement in the lives of their families.

Will we slow down and devote more time to family activity? Probably. The mood of the nation is such that all relationships, including those within the family, have assumed a renewed sense of importance. Our schedules will increasingly reflect that importance.

Currently, America is reacting against the models of womanhood put forth by feminist reformers in the sixties and seventies, the consequences of which have become more acute in the turbulent cultural upheaval of the eighties. As adults struggle to make sense of the changes that engulf them and try to slow their lives to a manageable pace, many are turning back to traditonal family ideas as one survival tactic.

Taking their cues from the Bible, Christians should define how a successful family allocates its time. Because God wants us to care most about people, rather than possessions or positions, Christians in America would do well to examine their own schedules to determine what their priorities actually are and then make them what they ought to be.

Churches, too, must rethink what they ask of individuals. Some people have told us that they believe their families suffer because the church expects them to devote too much of their free time to church-related activities. Others have noted that some church-sponsored "family" events actually split the family—one set of activities for parents, another for children, and perhaps yet another for teenagers. One church member commented, "I'd love it if our church would put on things that I can do with my kids, not simultaneous to what my kids are doing. Yeah, sometimes I need a break, and I'm grateful for things they offer which allow me to think and interact like an adult for a change. But more often the problem for me is that I don't get to share these times with my kids because I'm talking about kids with an adult class while my kid is off somewhere being a kid with the children of the other parents."

Notes

1. See "Family Time: What Parents Want," a news release from the Family Research Council, Washington, D.C., February 1991; and James Dobson and Gary Bauer, *Children at Risk* (Waco, Tex.: Word, 1989), 133.

2. This information is drawn from various Barna Research Group studies, including "Omnipoll 2–92" (conducted January 1992); George Barna, *What Americans Believe* (Ventura, Calif.: Regal, 1991); and George Barna, *The Frog in the Kettle* (Ventura, Calif.: Regal, 1990).

3. Ibid.

4. The Gallup Poll in question was cited in the July 1991 issue of *American Demographics*, 11.

5. Drawn from the "Family in America" survey, conducted by Barna Research Group, Ltd., in February 1992. The national random sample size was 1,009 adults.

6. Ibid.

7. Ibid.

8. Ibid.

9. Ibid.

10. These statistics are from *Statistical Abstract of the United States, 1991*, Dept. of Commerce, Bureau of the Census, Washington, D.C., 1991, table 643, p. 391.

11. See *Business Week* (8 June 1992), 74.

12. From "Money Income of Households, Families and Persons in the U.S.: 1990," Dept. of Commerce, Bureau of the Census, series P-60, #174, table 13.

13. Cited in *American Demographics* (February 1991), 14.

14. Cited in *Business Week* (8 June 1992), 74.

15. "Hyping the Decline," *Washington Post* (27 July 1987), B5.

16. From Arlie Hochschild, *The Second Shift* (New York: Viking, 1989); Lewis Coser et al., *Introduction to Sociology*, 2d ed. (San Diego: Harcourt Brace Jovanovich, 1987); and several Barna Research Group studies conducted in 1989, 1991, and 1992.

17. From a promotional mailing for the newsletter "*Marketing to Women*," 1991.

18. Hochschild, *The Second Shift*, 3.

19. See James Sweet and Larry Bumpass, "Young Adults' Views of Marriage, Cohabitation, and Family," paper #33 in the National Survey of Families and Households, published by the Center for Demography and Ecology, University of Wisconsin-Madison. Also cited was a promotional mailing for *American Demographics*, 1990.

20. See "Family in America" study by the Barna Research Group; Hochschild, *The Second Shift*; Sweet and Bumpass,"Young Adults' Views on Marriage, Cohabitation, and Family"; and "What Does It Cost to Mind the Kids," a statistical brief from the Census Bureau, October 1990.

21. The Roper data were cited in Debra Goldman, "Death in the Family," *Adweek* (7 October 1991), 10.

22. Frances Goldscheider and Linda Waite, *New Families, No Families?* (Berkeley, Calif.: Univ. of California Press, 1991), 11.

23. This Roper Poll was reported in the March 1989 issue of the *Ladies Home Journal* and was based upon 1,000 in-home interviews with a national sample of women.

24. See *American Demographics* (April 1991), 6.

25. The National Opinion Research Corporation study cited here is described most completely in Andrew Greeley's book, *Faithful Attraction* (New York: Tor, 1991).

26. "Family in America" survey, Barna Research Group.

CHAPTER TEN

FAITH AND FAMILY

Religion is vitally important to most Americans. But in the last two decades we have witnessed a major transformation of the American religious landscape. No longer do traditional Christian values shape Americans' thinking. Nor is it realistic to assume that most adults worship with others in a church on Sunday morning. Most people still describe themselves as "religious," but the meaning of that word, like that of "family," has changed considerably.

Americans are increasingly skeptical about organized religion. Televangelist scandals have not hurt the Christian cause nearly as much as the widely held perception that churches offer little of practical value to those who attend their services and programs. The inward-looking, self-satisfied local church causes people to reject consistent church involvement.

At the same time that people are turning their backs on local churches, more and more adults are embracing the belief that the Bible may contain the answers to their most perplexing questions about meaning and significance. Yet even though the Bible is central to the

Christian faith, Christianity itself is becoming a less pervasive force in America. Millions of adults are dropping out of Catholic and Protestant churches, and many of them find their way back to religion through non-Christian religions. These are tough times indeed for the Christian church.

EXPERIMENTING WITH NEW FAITHS

Adults today consider the church experience less useful and desirable than previous generations did. In place of the traditional Sunday morning routine, many opt for personalized exercises in spiritual exploration and development. Sunday school, midweek services, and evangelistic crusades are being replaced by more intimate gatherings, such as small groups that meet for discussion, Bible study, and prayer; house churches; and worship festivals.

This religious transformation is not simply a matter of Americans questioning old-fashioned rituals. Many adults are rejecting essential religious beliefs, too. Millions of spiritual seekers are cross-breeding orthodox Christian beliefs with Eastern and New Age practices. Highly personalized belief systems are springing up everywhere, systems in which religion has been customized to meet the emotional needs, spiritual inclinations, and personal ambitions of the individual.[1] The desire to have a successful family that is grounded in some kind of spiritual foundation has inspired many people to experiment with religion.

After a five-year period of experimentation, Boomers have been departing from churches in record numbers.

Take the experience of the Baby Boomers. One of the dominant reasons behind their return to churches in the late eighties was the desire to teach proper values and beliefs to their children. After years of marketing efforts aimed at attracting Boomers, churches at last struck a chord with Boomers who were searching for spiritual insight.

"I need help raising my kids, I admit it," said Stanton Williams. "Once I came to that realization, I fell back on what was familiar to me—the church. I was raised in it, though I don't know if it did much for me. But in a panic, my wife and I felt the church would be useful to us, so we went back. Big mistake." Williams and his family have departed from their church after a two-year stint. Instead, they now design their own Sunday and weeknight outings to clarify their values and beliefs about religious matters. "I know I'm not alone. Lots of my friends and coworkers have gone through the same disappointment over what the church has for us."

Churches expected the same programs and style of instruction that they had been using for years and years to satisfy the needs of these young adults. That expectation proved to be unrealistic. After a five-year period of experimentation, Boomers have been departing from churches in record numbers, starting in the early nineties. When churches offered only pat answers to increasingly complex issues, Boomers took their quest for spiritual enlightenment elsewhere. Sunday school, worship services, prayer chains, potluck dinners, and committee meetings simply did not address the needs of this maturing generation.[2]

Churches have also fumbled opportunities to draw in Baby Busters. Many people in this age group are strenuously searching for a new system of values to replace the self-serving system championed by the Baby Boomers. Busters generally feel that Boomers, by pursuing short-term, personal gain and exhibiting no care for, or deference to, the needs of later generations, have made a mess of things. Busters also reject the values of older generations. Their solution is to create an entirely new value system to live by.

In their search for answers, many young adults are turning to churches for help. Sadly, early research shows that few are finding the wisdom and guidance they want.[3] "It's been an empty experience for me so far," related Julia Somers. She was raised in a Presbyterian church, but has explored various Protestant and Catholic churches. "I assumed that I would find what I needed in a Christian church. That hasn't been my experience, though. They're virtually interchangeable, and none so far has shown me anything that is real or substantive. What's so strange is that all I'm really looking for is a way of seeing the world that holds together and isn't based on self-gain."

Americans tend to expect religion to tell them what is right and wrong, what is good and bad, how to succeed, and how to avoid failure. The church's failure to articulate answers to these fundamental questions in a consistent and positive manner has alienated many young adults. More than at any time in the recent past, Americans are relying on their own wisdom to define the role of religion in their lives.

THE INFLUENCE OF RELIGION

In general, adults believe that organized religion is losing its influence over people. Only one out of five adults believes that churches exert more influence on society than they did five years ago. By contrast, twice as many contend that churches actually have less influence than they did five years ago.[4]

At the same time, though, a majority of adults admit that their religious beliefs greatly affect their personal views on family-related matters. For instance, more than half of all adults say that their religious views have "a lot" of influence on their thinking about family, raising children, and marriage. Four out of ten say that those beliefs have influenced substantially their thoughts on sexual behavior. (See Table 10.2 for a summary of these findings.)

A majority also say that they believe the Bible has a lot of practical advice on how to have a successful marriage and family. Unfortunately, this belief appears to be superficial. Although most Americans have been raised in Protestant or Catholic homes and have spent a part of their life under the tutelage of a church, few of them have any idea what the Bible says about family matters. (Table 10.1 summarizes our findings.) This knowledge gap is also noticeable in other areas. For instance, despite the fact that 43 percent of respondents believe that the Bible has a lot of practical advice for single adults on ways of leading a successful and fulfilling life, most of the people answering in this way could not give an example of such advice.[5] (See Table 10.3 for the results of this survey question.)

| TABLE 10.1 | Religious Influence: Family and Marriage |

Religion and the Family
How much have your religious beliefs influenced your view of the family?

Percentage of people influenced

Group	A lot	Some	A little or none
All	52%	30%	17%
Currently married	56%	29%	15%
Never been married	42%	32%	26%
Divorced	47%	32%	19%
Widowed	71%	21%	6%
With children under 18	57%	28%	15%
Without children under 18	43%	34%	22%
White	51%	30%	18%
Black	63%	25%	12%
Hispanic	56%	32%	12%

Source: "Family in America" survey conducted in February 1992 by the Barna Research Group, Ltd. These data reflect the views of the 1,009 people interviewed in the study.

Religion and Marriage
How much have your religious beliefs influenced your view of marriage?

Percentage of people influenced

Group	A lot	Some	A little or none
All	53%	27%	15%
Currently married	57%	27%	15%
Never been married	40%	28%	30%
Divorced	48%	27%	24%
Widowed	68%	22%	6%
With children under 18	56%	27%	16%
Without children under 18	46%	26%	26%
White	51%	28%	20%
Black	70%	21%	10%
Hispanic	48%	27%	22%

Source: "Family in America" survey conducted in February 1992 by the Barna Research Group, Ltd. These data reflect the views of the 1,009 people interviewed in the study.

Nevertheless, religion still exerts considerable influence on the family. People who have been married, whether the marriage is still intact or has been dissolved through divorce or the death of a spouse, are much more likely to agree that religion influences their family views and behavior. (Table 10.1 displays the influence of religious views on marriage.) Adults who have never made a trip to the altar are nearly twice as likely to indicate that religious beliefs have had little or no effect on their family views.

Furthermore, adults who have had children are much more likely to say that religion has affected their family life than do those who have never had kids. "We frequently find that having children is such a life-transforming experience that adults grope for a way to understand what is happening to them," explained one marriage counselor who helps new parents adjust to life with infants. "Religion is one of the stabilizing forces with which they are acquainted. Often, they will turn to the religious group they knew as a child, in the hope that it will provide the direction and strength they feel lacking in themselves."(Table 10.4 looks at how effectively churches have helped parents in raising their children.)

Interestingly, it is the two largest ethnic groups—blacks and Hispanics—who agree most frequently that religion influences their family life. Notice in Table 10.1, for instance, that white adults were generally less likely than adults of color to say that religion has had a lot of influence on their thinking or views on raising children. The statistics also point out that black adults, in particular, say that religion has had a lot of impact on them.

It is also worth mentioning that religion has apparently had the least success in altering sexual behavior. In particular, those who have never been married, divorced adults, and those who do not have children tend to say that religion has had little affect on their sexual freedom. (This is particularly true of whites more than ethnic groups. See Table 10.2 for specific details.) Such a finding raises a disturbing question: How seriously do people long for religious guidance when they refuse to heed its advice in such a basic area of morality?

THE SUPPORTING ROLE OF THE CHURCH

It seems reasonable to conclude that many adults are rejecting the influence of religion on their families because past experiences have

| TABLE 10.2 |

Religious Influence: Children and Sex

Religion and Children

How much have your religious beliefs influenced your view of raising children?

Percentage of people influenced

Group	A lot	Some	A little or none
All	51%	28%	20%
Currently married	53%	20%	17%
Never been married	37%	30%	30%
Divorced	58%	24%	17%
Widowed	67%	19%	12%
With children under 18	57%	27%	16%
Without children under 18	37%	29%	29%
White	48%	30%	21%
Black	71%	15%	14%
Hispanic	51%	29%	18%

Source: "Family in America" survey conducted in February 1992 by the Barna Research Group, Ltd. These data reflect the views of the 1,009 people interviewed in the study.

Religion and Sexual Behavior

How much have your religious beliefs influenced your view of sexual behavior?

Percentage of people influenced

Group	A lot	Some	A little or none
All	40%	28%	32%
Currently married	41%	29%	30%
Never been married	31%	28%	41%
Divorced	33%	28%	27%
Widowed	53%	20%	24%
With children under 18	43%	27%	29%
Without children under 18	31%	29%	39%
White	37%	29%	33%
Black	59%	20%	21%
Hispanic	43%	29%	28%

Source: "Family in America" survey conducted in February 1992 by the Barna Research Group, Ltd. These data reflect the views of the 1,009 people interviewed in the study.

taught them that the church is of little help in times of need. Currently, fewer than half of all adults say that Protestant churches are very sensitive to the needs of families. Even more revealing is the fact that just one out of every six adults say that Protestant churches are very sensitive to the needs of single adults. Just as few (17 percent) describe those churches as being very sensitive to the needs of single parents.[6]

At the same time, however, a majority of adults view Christian churches as being very supportive of both men and women in the primary roles they play within a family. Two-thirds of all adults say that Christian churches support or assist women very well in their role as mother; three out of five say they support women in their role as wives; and half indicate that churches do very well at assisting women who take care of elderly parents. A similar two-thirds majority view Christian churches as providing a very strong level of support for men in their role as fathers; six out of ten say churches support them very well as husbands; but just one-third say that churches do a very good job at supporting men who are involved in caring for an elderly parent.[7]

How can these seemingly contradictory views—that churches are not very sensitive to the needs of families, singles, and single parents, but are supportive of men and women in their primary family roles—be reconciled?

The answer appears to lie in the tendency of churches to teach ideas rather than skills. For example, when parents with children under the age of eighteen were asked to rate how well churches and religious groups help them raise their children, only 36 percent said they found churches to be very helpful. This low evaluation indicates that most churches, for all their talk about the importance of parenting and nurturing children, do not provide the hands-on skills and other practical resources parents feel they need. "I don't come to hear sermons on how I must be a better, more caring parent," scolded one southern man with two teenagers. "I have enough guilt about what I'm not doing as a father. What I need is someone to help me see the problems, and especially the solutions, ahead of the crisis points I go through as a parent. That's what I need, not platitudes." Interestingly, it was the white community that

TABLE
10.3 # The Bible, Family, and Singleness

The Bible and Family
How much practical advice does the Bible have on marriage/family?
Percentage saying

Group	A lot	Some	A little or none
All	55%	27%	15%
Currently married	57%	28%	13%
Never been married	45%	28%	23%
Divorced	54%	26%	17%
Widowed	69%	18%	9%
With children under 18	58%	26%	13%
Without children under 18	47%	31%	20%
White	52%	29%	17%
Black	77%	12%	9%
Hispanic	58%	26%	14%

Source: "Family in America" survey conducted in February 1992 by the Barna Research Group, Ltd. These data reflect the views of the 1,009 people interviewed in the study.

The Bible and Singleness
How much practical advice does the Bible give on the successful single life?
Percentage saying

Group	A lot	Some	A little or none
All	43%	30%	22%
Currently married	44%	30%	20%
Never been married	34%	30%	33%
Divorced	46%	34%	14%
Widowed	59%	21%	15%
With children under 18	46%	29%	19%
Without children under 18	35%	32%	29%
White	41%	30%	23%
Black	66%	23%	11%
Hispanic	42%	30%	21%

Source: "Family in America" survey conducted in February 1992 by the Barna Research Group, Ltd. These data reflect the views of the 1,009 people interviewed in the study.

had the least favorable regard for churches on this issue.[8]

Churches and religious groups appear to be failing in the way they serve and care for single parents. Often, especially right after a divorce, single parents turn to a church for help, only to find that their marital status has in effect disqualified them from the fellowship. Studies on divorce invariably note that both the parents and children involved in the breakup of a family are in a very vulnerable, confused emotional state and require intensive care and acceptance in order to regain stability and self-esteem.[9]

Often, single parents and divorced adults feel abandoned by the churches they had attended. One woman poured out her frustration: "My divorce hit me like a freight train. I was emotionally paralyzed for months. Here I was, a faithful member at the church, and once word got around that I was now a divorced mother, I might as well have been a leper. Friends stopped calling, people avoided eye contact. It was horrible! Even the pastor reacted differently to me, kind of like he understood how tough it must be to be a public sinner or something. If I hadn't been so devastated by the divorce, realizing just how fragile my church relationships were would have been a major blow."

A major clinical study of divorced families reported that half of the couples involved in the study had been members or regular participants in the activities of a church or synagogue. During the period in which the family was contemplating the divorce, and during the crisis period immediately after the divorce was made legal, none of those family members received a personal, in-home visit by a clergy person.[10] In fact, research among the clergy suggests that they often have little experience in counseling couples with marital problems and may consequently avoid direct confrontation with such people.[11]

Fortunately, thousands of churches are now becoming more attuned to the need to provide the same openness and care for single parents that they offer to married adults. Many congregations are sponsoring divorce recovery groups, providing better training for church leaders who meet with single adults, and exhibiting a growing sensitivity to people in the throes of divorce. The future may be brighter for those who seek solace from churches in the wake of their failed marriages.

TABLE
10.4 | The Church and Raising Children

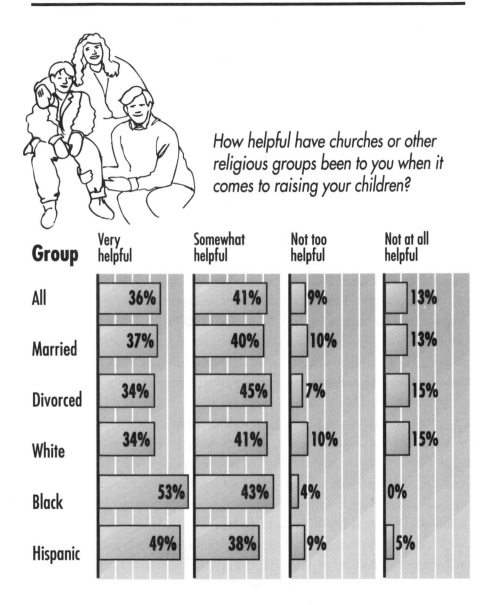

How helpful have churches or other religious groups been to you when it comes to raising your children?

Group	Very helpful	Somewhat helpful	Not too helpful	Not at all helpful
All	36%	41%	9%	13%
Married	37%	40%	10%	13%
Divorced	34%	45%	7%	15%
White	34%	41%	10%	15%
Black	53%	43%	4%	0%
Hispanic	49%	38%	9%	5%

Source: "Family in America" survey conducted in February 1992 by the Barna Research Group, Ltd. These data reflect only the responses of parents with children under the age of 18

In our consumer-oriented, market-driven society, more and more people evaluate major institutions on the basis of what practical value they have to offer. They tend to scrutinize religion—whether delivered through the local church, synagogue, or small group—in the same way. Since most adults no longer search actively for absolute truth, they frantically seek every morsel of wisdom that any individual or group can give that will help them make sense out of their lives. Because most adults want to get married and eventually have children, and because few individuals or social groups provide any wisdom or training for parenthood, adults are turning to the church for help with the tremendous responsibilities they face daily. But unless the church steps up its efforts to reach out to young adults, those needs may not be met.

THE PERSISTENCE OF RELIGIOUS FAITH

Despite the problems churches are experiencing, Americans continue to indicate that religion will continue to play a significant, if not leading, role in family-related matters. Currently, a majority of adults in America regularly attend some kind of religious meeting (such as church services, temple services, religious instruction classes) three or more times each month. Most families associate with a particular church: fewer than one out of every four families does not attend religious services at a regular place of worship.

The evidence also shows that a majority of adults engage in religious activity beyond the most obvious, public religious practices. Most adults say that they read from the Bible in a typical week. Two-thirds say that they enjoy praying to God and that they do so regularly. A majority of adults watch or listen to the messages communicated by Christian leaders on television or radio. About half of all adults commit some of their free time to reading religious books, magazines, or periodicals toward learning more about what religion (primarily Christianity) has to say about their daily struggles and eternal hopes.[12]

Millions of adults express hope that their churches will have a lasting impact on them and their families. In fact, when we asked adults who should be responsible for imparting values to their children, the answers included only three different responses: parents themselves (named by 98 percent), churches (56 percent), and schools (52 percent). Despite these hopes, their disheartening assessment is that churches won't have such an impact. When asked to identify who has the most influence on children's values these days, only 1 percent named churches— ranking them a distant fifth behind friends and peers of their children (33 percent), parents (30 percent), the mass media (21 percent), and schools (13 percent).[13]

Yet if we allow God's influence to permeate our families, real change can result. National Opinion Research Corporation studies have shown that shared prayer can be a powerful means of bonding between husband and wife, leading to a higher probability of a stable and enjoyable marriage. Other studies have indicated that the intensity with which adults accept basic biblical principles about marriage and family, such as the permanence of the union, the importance of bearing and raising children, the necessity of employing loving discipline, and the involve- ment within a supportive religious community can all reinforce family cohesion.[14]

HOW CHRISTIANS CAN RESPOND

Religion may not have the same influence in American society it once had. Traditional creeds obviously have less impact on the thinking and lifestyles of Americans. The fact remains, however, that most Americans are religious in some sense and consciously allow their religious beliefs to color some of their most important personal values and behavior.

The remainder of the nineties will likely find Protestant churches trying to back up their teaching about family with the action that addresses the serious practical needs of millions of families. People will be open to ministries that provide tangible help. In fact, how adequately a church responds to family needs may well determine how that church grows in the years ahead.

How can you be ready to meet those needs? First, reexamine your philosophy about family matters and try to discern how consistently these ideas mesh with your religious beliefs. Often adults hold views on child discipline, divorce, premarital sex, homosexuality, or abortion, for example, that are inconsistent with their Christian faith. Study God's

Word to correct any erroneous ideas you have picked up. Second, it might be fruitful to consider how your church could serve your family needs more effectively. Then alert your church leaders to those needs. Many churches struggle to identify how they can provide more valuable assistance to families. By helping the church's leaders understand your needs, you will likely increase the church's awareness of how it can serve not only your family, but all the families in your congregation.

Notes

1. For a more comprehensive discussion of cultural change and the role of the church in that change, see George Barna, *The Frog in the Kettle* (Ventura, Calif.: Regal, 1990); Leith Anderson, *Dying for Change* (Minneapolis: Bethany House, 1991); and Russell Chandler, *Racing Toward 2001* (San Francisco: Harper Collins, 1992).

2. A broader discussion of the Baby Boom attraction to and repulsion from churches appeared in "The Case of the Missing Boomers," in the April-June 1992 issue of "Ministry Currents," a quarterly newsletter published by the Barna Research Group.

3. A more comprehensive examination of the emotional and psychological turmoil of Baby Busters, and how religion pertains to their quest for meaning, is found in George Barna, *The Invisible Generation: Baby Busters* (Glendale, Calif.: Barna Research, 1992).

4. From "Omnipoll 2-92," conducted in July 1992 by Barna Research Group, Ltd.

5. Data from "Family in America" survey, conducted by Barna Research Group, Ltd., in February 1992. The national random sample size was 1,009 adults.

6. From "Omnipoll 2-91," conducted in July 1991 by the Barna Research Group, Ltd.

7. Ibid.

8. Ibid.

9. Ibid.

10. See Judith Wallerstein and Sandra Blakeslee, *Second Chances* (New York: Ticknor & Fields, 1989), 7.

11. From an unreleased study entitled "A View from the Pulpit," conducted in 1992 by the Barna Research Group, Ltd., among a national sample of Protestant church pastors.

12. Data from both "Omnipoll 1-92" (January 1992) and "Omnipoll 2-92."

13. "Family in America" survey, Barna Research Group.

14. Andrew Greeley cites the National Opinion Research Corporation conclusions in his book *Faithful Attraction* (New York: Tor, 1991). The relationship between the intensity and commitment of one's faith and the health of one's marriage and family are drawn from Barna Research studies conducted in 1991 and 1992. Specifically, evangelical Christians and their family views and experiences were compared to people with less religious commitment.

CHAPTER ELEVEN

STRENGTHENING THE FAMILY

The nineties are not going to be an easy time for the traditional family. Consider the forces lined up against it: ingrained public perceptions about the family's demise; selective media reporting that gives a favorable slant to alternative lifestyles; the politically correct movement that seeks to dismantle the traditional elements of the family; movies, music, and television programs that show families as divided and weak; schools that either refuse to or legally cannot teach traditional family views; churches that fail to provide for the practical needs of families; government policies that penalize traditional families and provide incentives to nouveau family experiments; and self-absorbed lifestyles. Given this array of combatants, it is nothing short of a miracle that we have any families left in America. Indeed, one might question whether it is even reasonable to expect that there will be traditional families in our future. The answer, however, is an unequivocal yes!

Here's why: marriage is the best system for protecting and nurturing spouses and their children. No alternative has been developed—

and many have been tried—that meets the needs of its partners so completely. Above all else, most people want to live happily ever after, satisfying their dreams and fantasies with as little pain and sacrifice as possible. Like all relationships, marriages inevitably develop challenges that require the partners to compromise and reconsider some of their ambitions, but marriage is an ingenious arrangement because it compels the partners to commit to each other and to work through those problems together. We must not forget that marriage works primarily because it was created and ordained by God as the best means of joining men and women together. He has not changed His mind about the wisdom of this plan for building human relationships, raising children, and fostering mutual support.

Nevertheless, marriage will continue to face an onslaught of pressures and challenges. Divorce will remain popular because Americans are prone to pursue selfish desires, regardless of the long-term consequences. Although there are some instances in which a divorce may be the only way out of an abusive or adulterous relationship, we have made the exception into the rule. Because of the empty values of American culture, we can anticipate that the current unacceptably high rate of divorce will remain essentially unchanged during the nineties. Cohabitation, neglect of families, selfishness, sexual promiscuity, easy divorce, and the widespread expectation of marital disaster will result in yet more broken promises and dissolved relationships.

Experimentation in all realms of life is both normal and desirable. However, when an experiment fails, it is necessary to pull the plug on that test and learn the lesson it imparted. If we imagine all of the nouveau family designs as being test cases against which we were to compare our control group (the traditional family), then the dismal results of this experiment must compel us to acknowledge publicly that many of the nouveau systems fail to provide even a fraction of the security and benefits that the traditional family can offer.

The failure of nouveau families to provide the level of contentment its proponents have expected is largely due to the absence of accepted and respected boundaries for behavior. Role confusion is rampant. Most nouveau families are ambiguously put together and are frequently unstable. Dealing with crises is difficult because there is no source of authority to fall back upon. Responsibilities that one family member finds unappealing often go undone because that person is free to set his or her own standards of behavior. An anything-goes philosophy reigns. In the end, individuals become committed solely to self-gratification; anarchy results, and the family dissolves.

Marriage will prevail precisely because it delivers the greatest degree of personal satisfaction and stability. The question is, how do we get from where we are today to a condition in which we have to go through less pain and suffering, less trial and error, to realize the benefits available through a strong family?

ADVICE FOR SINGLE ADULTS

There is no biblical support for the notion that a person is incomplete if he or she is not married. In fact, the Bible suggests that remaining single can be a gift from God if it is accompanied by a celibate lifestyle and devoted service to God.

But most single adults desire a life partner, and most will wind up marrying at some point. What can we learn from the experience of those who have been through the process? An important step toward finding the right mate is to identify and scrutinize the underlying expectations. Are they reasonable? Do they fit with your true needs and future goals? The assumptions that you bring into a relationship will affect that relationship's long-term health.

Creating a family is an important responsibility and opportunity. It is not a disposable relationship.

To identify your expectations, then, it is also helpful to identify your fundamental needs and priorities. Often, the lifestyles and relationships we pursue conflict because we have not clearly thought them through. Once you have identified the principles in life you cannot compromise, build them into your description of the kind of person you would like to marry. For instance, Christians would be well advised to accept the Bible's admonition not to be "unequally yoked"—that is, not to marry non-Christians. Determining what you would value most highly in your prospective partner will enhance the probability of successfully identifying that person.

Another lesson learned by many married people is that in most cases there is no virtue to hurrying into a marriage. Time reveals much about a relationship. Take the required time to understand each other thoroughly; to discuss goals in life and what types of sacrifices might be required to reach those goals, and how committed each of you really is to such sacrifices. You should recognize ahead of time that marriages often go through a cycle of romance, routine, and restlessness. As you reflect on your relationship, think about how you would handle such changes with your prospective spouse. The romance stage is always the most intense and alluring, but it is usually the most short-lived, too. Take the time to figure out what the relationship might ultimately be like under the various circumstances you experience in life.

A final consideration is the value of gaining outside perspectives and assistance. Seek the counsel of other people whom you can trust to offer an honest and loving assessment of the relationship. Study the experiences of others to determine what has made for healthy families, and whether or not the relationship in which you're involved offers a good chance of developing those healthy traits. And don't leave God out of the picture. Pray for His guidance and see what you can discover about yourself and your relationship by examining the Bible's wisdom.

Creating a family is an important responsibility and opportunity. It is not a disposable relationship. Do whatever you can to make a wise decision in choosing a partner, for it is one of the most important steps of your life.

ADVICE FOR MARRIED ADULTS

Much research has been done on the attributes of strong families. The results have been surprisingly consistent. What is perhaps even more surprising, though, is how consistently we ignore the lessons of that research.

For instance, one survey identified what most Americans say would help strengthen marriages. People believe that appropriate strategies include families' openly sharing their needs and desires with each other; sharing activities with each other, such as recreational times and household chores; having times of family prayer; taking vacations together as a family; and sharing religious activities in addition to prayer. Interestingly, if you study the pressures and problems that typically precede a divorce, it seems that the solutions enumerated above would go far toward heading off many marital splits. Investing ourselves in these types of efforts while the family is relatively strong would be in the best interests of all.

Other research has brought to light a dozen or so characteristics of strong families. These attributes have been identified by a number of different researchers. The consistency of the results, despite the various research approaches used, underscores their likely validity. The ingredients common to most strong families appear to include:

- strong, supportive, honest communication
- a significant quantity of time spent together
- shared religious faith and practice
- agreement on key values
- love, consideration, understanding, mutual appreciation
- common interests, goals, and purposes
- ability to positively negotiate solutions to crises
- commitment to deepening the intrafamily relationships
- optimism about the stability of the family
- a firm parental coalition in dealing with children
- regular sexual intercourse with the spouse
- willingness to sacrifice personal interests and resources for the good of the family
- behavior that earns the trust of family members (for instance, sexual fidelity, financial integrity, and so on)[1]

No one would be foolish enough to suggest that such outcomes can be easily achieved. Having a functional, healthy family is hard work.

It requires perhaps more commitment than any other endeavor in a person's life. Research has demonstrated that it is possible to achieve a strong family—and that it is worth the effort.

WHAT YOU CAN DO TO ENHANCE FAMILY LIFE IN AMERICA

It all starts with you. The family in our society will only be as strong as you, and others like you, make it. Here are a few additional thoughts you might consider if you want to strengthen your family in the midst of a culture that is seemingly hostile to the traditional family.

Encourage balance in life. Our society encourages people to achieve; God encourages people to "be." What does He want us to be? Exactly what He designed us to become: happy, healthy, worshipful, fulfilled individuals who have a proper perspective on life. The only means to grasping that perspective is to achieve balance in the variety of tasks we take on each day.

The typical adult has to juggle a multitude of tasks: work, family, friends, leisure, faith, material needs, physical needs, and more. A valuable step toward figuring out how to balance competing opportunities and priorities is to develop a philosophy of life or worldview that puts these elements into perspective.

Most Americans do not have a philosophy of life. This missing component renders them powerless to overcome the tyranny of the urgent. Decisions are made without an understanding of what is and is not important; we often fail to see what are the best means for accomplishing our life goals (if we have identified such goals). Until we can create a mental map of what is important to us, the chances that we will arrive at a fulfilling destination are minimal.

Educate your children at home. Parents, in particular, must consider the importance of educating their children with the basic building blocks of character. This means that before the schools, the media, and a child's playmates have the chance to radically influence a son or daughter in ways that tear down what parents are hoping to build up, the parents must take the initiative and educate their children in critical areas of life, using the Bible as the ultimate authority. Church, schools, and other sources of assistance and guidance should be secondary influences, reinforcing rather than introducing fundamental beliefs and values. The family ought to be the place from which a child develops his or her ideas about materialism, sexuality, relationships, and family and civic responsibilities.

The church must proclaim God's view of family.

Participate in the political process. Every adult also has both the privilege and responsibility to influence local, state, and federal legislation that will dictate the environment in which a family lives. If more Christians let their elected officials know their feelings about such matters as divorce, abortion, child abuse, alimony, values clarification, public education, discipline, and litigation against parents, the law of the land would be quite different. Lacking the input of people who believe in the worth of traditional families—in many cases those who have wrongly assumed that their interests were being protected by elected officials—government has responded instead to the people seeking to challenge bibically based values. The only way to protect the freedoms we possess, and to restore some of those that have been removed, is to get involved in the political process—through letters and calls to officials, by voting, attending town meetings, joining advocacy groups, and praying for God's blessing and direction in the political process.

WHAT YOUR CHURCH CAN DO TO HELP THE FAMILY
There are more than 300,000 churches spread across the land that purport to love and serve Jesus Christ. If that is so, each of those churches must be involved in efforts to support the family that He designed and loves to this day. Every Christian, whether presently holding a leadership position in the church or not, can help his or her church support the traditional family in America in the ways described in the paragraphs that follow.

Teach God's views. The church must proclaim God's view of family. This means publicizing the virtues of the traditional family and alerting adults to the disastrous effects that will emerge if we continue to tolerate the nouveau family. The Christian church can clarify the key points of the debate and provide people with practical responses to the battle now being waged.

Many people fail to understand the ramifications of our nation's acceptance of alternative lifestyles. If the church fails to inform people of the dangers, the chances are good that most people will never be exposed to the truth. The Bible clearly spells out God's expectations regarding family. It is the obligation of church leaders to ensure that their congregations are well-informed about those truths.

Support families. The church is the only institution left in our society that consistently speaks out for family values. Using the Bible as the guidebook, Christians can and should create a compelling argument for why we need families, what a strong family looks like, and how the church, as a community of people with shared beliefs, can help its respective families achieve their potential within a traditional family structure. This means offering people more than just solid teaching about family (although that's an integral element, too). Churches might consider the value of the following:

- sponsoring programs that educate young people about family matters, including God's views on sexuality
- developing systems through which teenagers who become pregnant can be assured of a good home for a child if they do not want to raise it, thus reducing the likelihood of abortion
- providing healthy and uplifting entertainment and activities for young people to counter the disturbing ideas pushed at them in the media
- offering adults tangible models of what healthy families look like and of the commitment it takes to maintain a godly family
- providing strong, biblical teaching on God's intentions for the family, the role of the church in supporting families, and how God tells us to deal with family difficulties and crises

- installing pastors, church staff, and lay leaders only if they have healthy, strong family lives (in fact, the apostle Paul in 1 Timothy includes this standard as one of the important qualifications for church leaders)
- publicly, forcefully, and intelligently addressing erroneous ideas that have gained wide currency—such as the notion that cohabitation serves as an insurance policy against divorce, the belief that half of all marriages end in divorce, the 10 percent myth regarding homosexuality, the belief that children rebound from divorce better than adults, and so on
- offering homemakers options that will enable them to use their talents for productive, in-home enterprises that eliminate the need to work outside the home
- developing financial and employment assistance for church families going through difficult times
- supporting adults so strongly that when a marriage is endangered, the church becomes a primary support system, providing encouragement, counseling, prayer support, and the other forms of assistance needed to protect the family
- supporting adults and children from broken families so that they may rebuild their lives in an environment of love and understanding, rather than in isolation, condemnation, and poverty
- adequately motivating and educating Christians, who can in turn influence the political leaders who draft and vote on family policy

Carrying out these programs requires that ministries work together, across denominational and doctrinal lines, for the good of the family. Churches will need to make a determined effort in an era of insufficient resources and media hostility to protect traditional lifestyles. And to see these efforts bear fruit will necessitate more than just a few classes in which people talk about the ideal family. Many adults have told us, in survey after survey, that churches give lip service to the needs of families but never roll up their sleeves and deal with the tough stuff that families really struggle with. If we are serious about the church being a place of love, understanding, support, and assistance, we must convert our local congregations into activist organizations that commit massive resources to serving families.

A NEW CONSENSUS

Some analysts have wondered aloud whether it is even possible in a pluralistic society like ours to arrive at a consensus about the meaning and worth of family. I think it is.

Let's assume that by "pluralistic society" we mean a population in which many competing viewpoints are allowed to coexist. American society is pluralistic because people may believe whatever they wish; they may live, within relatively loose legal limitations, however they desire; and they may espouse whatever political and social perspectives they choose to champion. Should we expect, then, that Americans will all agree on the meaning, the role, and the design of family? No. In fact, in a healthy democratic society, we should encourage all sides to contribute to the debate, praying that God will supply wisdom to the people so they may arrive at the best possible options. A society that squelches debate is a society in danger of losing its grasp on the truth. In the the same way, a government that imposes a "consensus" on its citizens is no longer free—just ask the people who suffered in Stalin's Russia or Hitler's Third Reich. If our national history shows nothing else, it proves that the democratic process allows us to resolve conflict for the good of society.

How then is it possible to achieve consensual support for the traditional family? We must keep in mind American society had for decades what amounted to a consensus about family matters. Only during the upheaval of the sixties and seventies was this consensus shattered. It will take hard work and prayer, but the consensus can be restored again. To do so, we must persuade people to recognize the wisdom of family values and the hope they offer for restoring broken families and creating strong, new ones. And who are the people we must persuade? Mainly, the influential people who determine business, govermental, religious, and educational policy. Specifically, we should point to five groups.

Politicians. Politicians are taught to be responsive to the public will. If they sense a groundswell of individuals who refuse to accept the status quo and who can articulate a clear vision for the future, they will be forced to listen to their demands. Politicians who are pro-family can lead the way in forming a new consensus in America.

Clergy. Christian pastors and clergy form the vast majority of the religious leadership in America. They are motivated to please God by teaching and counseling people with His Word, thereby helping them live successfully. Christian leaders should put aside denominational differences and work together to arrive at a consensus about what constitutes a family system that honors God. Once this consensus has been reached, Christians must form a united front to defend these principles in the public arena.

Business leaders. Typically, corporate leaders are responsible to their stockholders. Their bottom line is dominated by financial outcomes. They generally acknowledge that what serves the best interests of the society will most likely reap the greatest financial rewards for them. Christians should encourage corporations to act responsibly and to develop products and services that will strenghten families. Business leaders can easily arrive at a consensus by recognizing that what is best for the families of the nation is, in the end, best for their business interests.

The media. Access to information is central to a free society. When the media do their job well—that is, objectively reporting what they find, without unsolicited or acknowledged editorializing—they have no vested interest in shaping a new consensus or supporting an old one. Their role in not to be a decision-maker, but to provide unbiased and accessible information to those who are responsible for the decisions. Christians must demand fair and accurate treatment of family issues.

Educators. Teachers are responsible to provide people with the skills and information that will enable them to make wise decisions and to live as productive and loyal citizens. Can educators come to a consensus about family? Given the enormous responsibility that they have for caring for and nurturing the development of young minds, it is in their best interests to arrive at a consensus about what would most enhance the development of young people, and to educate those youths about such values. If part of the function of our educational system is to transmit a common heritage to the upcoming generation, then that system must understand and pass along a common view of family. Christians need to help educators realize that the problems they witness in the classroom could be lessened if traditional values were once again communicated.

When the restoration of family values becomes the object of a widespread, national campaign, it is likely that a consensual understanding of family will be achieved. Indeed, the history of the United States shows that this nation has survived because it is practical. Despite the acceptance of nouveau families, Americans retain a deep sense that all is not well with the values they have embraced. Christians have the capacity to respond to those concerns intelligently. We, however, must summon the will to persevere in the long, hard battle ahead. If we do, we will bestow on future generations an invaluable legacy.

Notes

1. Elizabeth Morgan, "Pioneer Research on Strong, Healthy Families," Family Research Council, Washington, D.C., no date; "Free to Be Family," Family Research Council, Washington, D.C., 1992; Andrew Greeley, *Faithful Attraction* (New York: Tor, 1991).